SUCCESSFUL FUNDRAISING

John Baguley

bibliotek books

First edition 1996

Grateful thanks are due to many charities who have supported the production of this book by granting us permission to reproduce examples of their campaign literature, in particular, Amnesty International, but also; St Christopher's Fellowship, Shelter, Greenpeace, Oxfam, British Red Cross, the Medical Foundation for the Care of Victims of Torture, the Royal Society for the Prevention of Cruelty to Animals and their advertising agency Abbott Mead Vickers BBDO Ltd. Thanks are also due to Bryan McAllister and *The Guardian* newspaper.

Published by
Bibliotek Books,
19 Warwick Road,
Stafford ST17 4PD, UK
ISBN 1 873017 15 4

Introduction

Confronted by the media with a daily diet of suffering and misery our natural response is to cry 'Surely something must be done to stop this?'. But while there are many things which can be done, they require resources, both human and financial. Human resources are needed to solve the immediate problem, and also to campaign for permanent change, and financial resources are needed not only to oil the wheels of change but to start the wheels turning in the first place. Fortunately the search for financial resources often delivers human resources as well. The search for such resources is one of the great challenges of our age and this book offers a blueprint for it.

It sets out a simple comprehensive framework upon which the details of your fundraising programme can be built. It then tackles each aspect of fundraising so that you can either build a programme or pick and mix ideas. The book arose out of a series of workshops given over several years, on behalf of a number of organisations, to fundraisers in Europe, Asia, the Pacific Rim and Africa. Copying my slides, overhead transparencies and notes to delegates never seemed adequate to meet more than their superficial needs. Inevitably, once the basic concepts had taken root and practical work started, a thousand new questions arose.

In place of marathon seminars and training workshops, I offer this book. As it is based largely on my own experiences it is heavily weighted in favour of the kind of fundraising that involves generating mass support for organisations, retaining that support and developing it over the years. It is particularly suited to pressure groups and campaigns where an extensive membership can also further organisational goals. Where this kind of fundraising involves closely following the wishes of the donors it has become known as relationship fundraising.

Naturally, a book will never entirely replace dialogue and the external environment is constantly changing. So, those readers who may want specialist advice or to respond to questions raised by this book can contact me on the Internet on http://www.city.ac.uk/~bh543/fundraising/services/ifc/index.html

I would like to acknowledge the invaluable assistance of the many fundraisers who assisted in the compilation of this book and who provoked many of the best thoughts that went into it. Any mistakes are, however, all my own.

Thanks are also due to my family, the Fundraising Department of Amnesty International British Section including Andy Hackman, Howard Lake, Craig Methven, Noreen O'Donaghue, Joanna Gilson, Alison Sanderson, Karen Sherlock; the Fundraising Working Group; Bjorn Andreassen, Luc Henkinbrant and John Lind Madsen; friends and fellow fundraisers Diana Chambers, Kalyan Singh Gupta, Han Juo-mei, Akira Ishihara, and Azusa Michida. Thank you!

John Baguley, Taipei, 1995

Contents

1 Developing a Fundraising Strategy

Fundraising is like the snow on Mount Fuji - it is often the most visible part of an organisation and the part that people notice first, but below the snow is the structure of the organisation carrying out its work. Holding the whole operation together over time is its strategy. Part and parcel of that overall strategy should be the fundraising strategy. This chapter shows not only the process by which it is created, but also the planning and budgeting that follow closely from a good strategy and ensure that it succeeds.

Setting a strategy

To be efficient in the search for funds it is necessary to plan, and to plan efficiently it is essential to have a strategy. That strategy will consist of selecting the best combination of fundraising techniques for your organisation and deploying them in close combination with the activities of the rest of the organisation, such as promotional or campaigning work. This helps to ensure that the organisation works harmoniously towards its overall goals. Fundraising is often seen as an add-on extra to an organisation's work, or as a necessary evil. Integrating the fundraising strategy into the overall work of the organisation will help change this attitude, reducing stress for the fundraisers and helping to maximise income generation.

An essential part of fundraising strategy is the allocation of resources

"My administration costs and overheads are absolutely nil. Every penny of your donation will go towards a cup of tea."

Reproduced by kind permission of The Guardian and Bryan McAllister.

1

to fundraising techniques to meet the organisation's need for income over time. Different techniques are needed to meet immediate needs, mid-term (say three- to five-year) needs and long-term (say five- to ten-year) needs. It is essential that short-term needs do not preclude investment in medium- or long-term strategies if income is to be maximised in the medium or long term. An important part of the work of anyone responsible for fundraising strategy is that they communicate the benefits of appropriate investment to those who allocate resources, so that the future needs of the organisation can be met as they occur.

Strategic thinking: getting started

If you have just started as a fundraiser in a charity, or if it is time to take stock of where your work is going, a good idea is to borrow a technique for strategic thinking from business management, called 're-engineering'. This has been called the blank page process. Take a blank page and write out where your organisation wants to be in three years time (or five years, or whatever timespan is appropriate) in terms of the income you will be required to generate. From that starting point calculate how you will generate that income as if you were starting from a greenfield site and not from the awful mess you may be confronted with at present. It is surprising what a salutary experience this exercise can be.

Knowing where the organisation would like to be in terms of the work it does, and hence what kind of financial resources will be required, means you can work out how much investment is needed in various areas of fundraising to produce those resources. Naturally, the resources may not be currently available and you may have to trim your investment, thus limiting future income growth. To do all this professionally it is essential to have an overview of the range of fundraising techniques that could be employed to reach your goals.

Reviewing the techniques: where the money comes from

Sources of funds are limited in number. They can be roughly grouped into the following categories: funds from individuals, governments, companies, trusts and foundations, the National Lottery (in the UK), trading, interest and dividends. Of course, funds from individuals come via a huge number of routes. As will be explained in detail later, many voluntary organisations' core funding comes in relatively small donations from many supporters (see Fig 1). Interest and dividends are not usually the responsibility of

1992 Charitable Giving by Source (in $ millions)		
Individuals	101,830	81.9%
Bequests	8,150	6.6%
Foundations	8,330	6.7%
Corporations	6,000	4.8%
Total	124,310	100.0%

Fig. 1 *Statistics from the Chronicle of Philanthropy, USA.*

fundraisers, though just as in the commercial world, the treasury function of charities is increasingly being scrutinised for efficiency as well as safety of investment.

Developing your strategy

Audit

To determine what techniques and resources you currently have at your disposal and how effective these are, the first thing to do is to undertake a thorough fundraising audit. This should list all the fundraising activities the organisation is now undertaking and critically appraise them. Who is responsible, how much is invested and how much earned? Comparative figures going back a few years will be essential in order to see if these activities are declining or improving and to make a projection forward. These extrapolations customarily assume that current trends continue unless there are good reasons to think otherwise. To check for such good reasons, it is necessary to look at the external environment as well as your organisation's internal operation.

Check the likely changes that may affect your organisation and its fundraising with regard to social, technological, economic, environmental and political factors - a STEEP analysis. You may find that investment in fundraising could be better deployed over the whole range of techniques to give a higher return on investment (ROI) but remember that some techniques can add synergy to your efforts. For example, national press advertising helps to build profile, and trading often helps local groups to create a feeling of belonging. These latter points are often hotly debated and you will need to form a view perhaps based partly on discussions with supporters. Is ROI everything ?

Gap analysis

The next step is to list which areas of fundraising are missing (gap analysis) and the costs and likely benefits of beginning those activities. This book will form a guide to the range of possibilities available to most fundraisers. Armed with this knowledge, a ranking should be made of all the possible areas of investment in terms of their short- and long-term cost-effectiveness, so that you and the organisation can decide how much of its scarce resources to devote to which areas of fundraising.

Making projections

It must be borne in mind throughout this exercise that maximising income in the long term requires investment at an initial loss, so the projections of possible future income from each source should run three to five years into the future.

Income from your donor-base

Essential steps in your strategy are to

- calculate future projections by estimating how many financial supporters (your donor-base) the organisation will have in each year of the projection. Donors can be called members, supporters, or friends, but their key characteristic is that they pay an annual fee or make a regular donation, and are therefore liable to give again if asked, always providing you have looked after them and built a relationship that met their needs.

- use the average number of donors to indicate future income from appeals, raffles, trading, etc., as the income from these activities is directly related to the number of donors you have (and their giving capacity). Multiply the average donation by the projected number giving in each case.

- reflect on the impact of inflation on your projection, and any other economic indicators agreed with your organisation's treasurer or finance officer.

In using the blank sheet of paper principle to determine where you wish to be in a few years time, it is necessary to

- estimate the number of supporters you will need in your final year. This tells you the bulk of your income for that year (add likely income from events, grants from trusts, shop income and other non-supporter income).

- work backwards from this estimate to calculate the investment needed each year to 'buy' those supporters. This will be based on the number of new members per thousand pounds invested in each recruitment activity (prospecting) such as direct mail, advertising or leaflets.

- take care not to assume that the market for new supporters is infinite. (Amnesty International, for example, has had difficulty recruiting new members through advertisements placed outside the Guardian, Independent and Observer newspapers. Friends of the Earth has undergone a vast and rapid period of growth and almost as rapid a period of decline, as the green movement's media exposure rose and fell dramatically.) However, the limits to growth are difficult to estimate, and it is easiest to look at other organisations in your field and determine their level of support as a benchmark or target for your organisation.

- work out how much to invest in 'buying' each new donor. For this, you need two vital pieces of information: the average 'lifetime' of a donor with you, and the amount they are likely to give over that lifetime. It is not as easy as it seems to calculate these numbers. The average lifetime of a donor will depend on the drop-out rate, ie. how many donors cease to support you each year. In a membership organisation you may have this information to hand, but if your organisation is increasing or decreasing rapidly the calculation is still not straightforward.

The average amount a donor is likely to give depends on the total income from all donors (this figure will come from a consideration of all those sources of income that depend directly on the supporters such as raffles, trading, direct mail appeals and legacies), less the total amount you spend on them per person in terms of newsletters, administration, new members' packs, etc.

Working backwards from future needs - an example

If your organisation has 20,000 members in the year 2001, bringing in £200,000 per year, and it will need to spend £550,000 in 2005, then in 2005 you will need 55,000 members, (unless you are absolutely sure of developing alternative sources of income). Can this be achieved?

If 10% of your members leave each year you will need to acquire the following new members each year:

	2002	2003	2004	2005
Start of year	18,000	34,200	48,780	61,902
Add in year	20,000	20,000	20,000	
Total at end	38,000	54,200	68,780	

which will give you a margin of error of better than 10%. Over four years this would be most welcome!

This is a simplified example with no account taken of inflation or other changes in the economy, or increases in membership fees or average donations. I have also ignored new members arriving during 2005, and, for clarity, assumed people all leave at the end of the year.

So the investment now needed is enough to bring in 20,000 new members each year, plus the full costs of servicing those members and appealing to them for extra funds. Is this available?

If a member stays with you for six years on average, and contributes £30 per year on average, in total they are worth (6 x £30) = £180 over their 'lifetime' with you. If the newsletter costs £4 per head per year and all other servicing costs £3 per head per year, then the member would cost (6 x £7) = £42 over their 'lifetime'. So each member is worth (£180 - £42) = £138 to you.

If an advertisement campaign costs £10,000 and brings in 100 members with an average donation of £18 your immediate loss will be £8,200. Over, say, the next six years these members will bring in (100 x £138) = £13,800 showing a long-term profit of £5,600. The question you must now ask is, 'Is this too close for comfort?'

If, instead, 200 people joined, the immediate loss would be (£10,000 - (200 x £18)) = £6,400, but over six years they would bring in (200 x £138) = £27,600 and yield a profit of £21,200. Is this more acceptable?

If, say, 400 people joined, the immediate loss would be (£10,000 - (400 x £18)) = £2,800, but over six years they would bring in (400 x £138) = £55,200 and generate a profit of £52,400. Do you have a more profitable and secure way of raising funds?

Fig. 1a *Planning and investment to meet future investment needs.*

Income from other sources

If substantial amounts of your income are from other sources such as the government, trusts, shops or events, the future may be more difficult to gauge.

Government policy can change overnight, and the State is in retreat from making provision for the voluntary sector in many Western countries. In fact, the current boom in voluntary sector enterprise is largely the result of attempts to replace previous government provision for various social services by charitable activity. During this retreat there have been some legal changes that benefit non-governmental organisations (NGOs), albeit principally those that are registered charities, by improving the range of donations on which a charity can reclaim the tax already paid. Improvements in the law relating to Gift Aid, Covenants and Payroll Giving are examples of this. Pay careful attention to changes in the National Budget which may affect your organisation's income. If your organisation is receiving funds directly from government sources it will know quite accurately the immediate and medium-term prospects for additional income.

Trusts do not usually like to make any long-term commitments which tie up their disposable income for years to come, and prefer to wean charitable organisations into becoming self-supporting. This is often a condition of any trust grant which lasts more than one year. Trust giving is rarely the mainstay of a large, long-lasting organisation. If this is the case with your organisation, it is particularly vulnerable and should be investing in alternative forms of income generation. Small pressure groups with few national supporters are often in this position, and can fold when their trust income dries up. It may be prudent to discuss this with your principal funders.

Shops can generate an excellent income, but you must allow for peaks and troughs. A prudent fundraising strategy will also develop other effective means of raising income as a hedge against the days when shops do badly or there is some unforeseen shift along the product cycle and people will no longer enter 'charity' shops.

New Sources

If your gap analysis indicates you should be investing in new areas of fundraising, it will help to discuss these with an experienced fundraiser or consultant to estimate possible income.

Having selected your range of techniques and put these together in a strategy you will need to budget to cover this cost and estimate how much income it will generate over time. Next, plan who does what. This will be essential in turning your strategy into reality. Most of this work will have been done as you selected and marshalled your techniques. You will probably find this to be an iterative process in which you will need to make many adjustments before you come up with an optimum strategy, which will then need to be agreed officially with your organisation before you have the green light to proceed.

Testing your strategy

In presenting a new strategy, particularly one involving increased investment or the introduction of new fundraising techniques into your organisation, you may well find that there is a strong tendency to think that it will only work for someone else.

'It won't work here'

It may work in London - but not in Wales, Scotland, or Rutland. It may work for Oxfam, Friends of the Earth and Save the Children - but we are different. It may work in India, Japan and Chile - but it won't work in Canada...

Phrases like these are so familiar to fundraisers that they have developed a stock response—test it! Naturally, there will be some cultural adaptation from country to country or organisation to organisation, but there is also a remarkable level of similarity of response around the globe to fundraising techniques. Schools' sponsored walks work for HelpAge International in India, Africa and Latin America. Direct mail works in Germany, India and Japan. Telemarketing works everywhere there is a phone.

Testing everything is a central tenet of good fundraising practice. It is at its most important in direct mail work. Here it is quite possible for you to test even the difference made in the response by a comma in one place or a comma in another place, by splitting the mailing list into two equal, random sets of people and mailing each of these two sets with a slightly different letter (coding the reply coupon differently for each). Of course, more significant things than commas are tested. In fact, so much has been tested so carefully that direct mail letters often bear a frightening similarity to each other.

If your organisation lacks a significant variety of income sources or is neglecting just one important technique, then try out a new idea on as small a scale as possible (always provided the results will be statistically significant) and, if it works, roll it out on a grand scale. It is important to maintain this practice in all your fundraising, as far as possible, as the years go by, and not to get set in your ways.

Testing new techniques, innovating and developing old techniques to keep them working and relevant to the changing market, all take time, research and enthusiasm; but that effort will be repaid by the results. Sometimes the difference will be sufficient to make a whole programme profitable, but though it may be worthwhile as an investment, obtaining resources is much harder if the programme makes even a small loss. In time the response to all ideas and materials runs down, and the best ideas become unprofitable unless renewed; but it often takes very little imaginative thought to revive a programme and regain a healthy return.

Budgeting

The importance of budgeting

I was once offered a fundraising position with a fairly large organisation, which was undertaking some unusual and interesting work on environmental issues, on the basis that, as a fundraiser, I should be able to raise my own salary and quite a bit more. On the face of it that seemed reasonable, but when I enquired how much the annual expenditure budget was to do this they said, 'Oh, what we meant was you must find the money to pay your own salary and then any money you need to spend on fundraising.' I did not accept the position.

Expenditure on fundraising is an essential part of any organisation's outgoings and fundraisers, like any other employees, should have a reasonable and secure income. The lack of proper budgeting for this is quite common, and sadly, this means that organisations do not grow at the rate they should and their charitable work is therefore severely curtailed. It is a false economy in any sector of business to underinvest in marketing the products, or in the research and development of those products.

Making budget adjustments

A proper budget gives you a clear idea of how much to spend on each of the projects that will be undertaken during the year or years ahead, and how much income is expected from each of those projects. Usually these will be on separate lines of the budget, and each month an account will be produced to show how the income and expenditure has gone on each of these lines (the management accounts) so that adjustments can be made to activities if they are over- or under-performing. Most years will see changes taking place with regard to expected income. Expenditure is much easier to predict, and, of course, no-one should overspend their budget without reference to higher authority. A dynamic organisation will immediately respond to this by investing heavily in those aspects of fundraising that are going well and reducing or ceasing expenditure on those areas that are not.

This is a very difficult area in which to take decisions, and mature experience is needed to understand exactly why an area of work is not performing as expected, and whether this is a temporary fluctuation or likely to be a permanent state of affairs. Naturally you need much more information than is provided in the management accounts to operate effectively, and this is covered in the 'Planning' sub-section under 'Fundraising reports'.

Budgeting for a single event

Most of your budgeting will be done for activities for which you have a track record. Towards the end of your financial year you may look back and see that you have held a flag day, organised a concert, run a direct mail programme and made four appeals to your organisation's supporters for extra funds. Next year, if things are going well, you will probably want to repeat those activities and organise some new ones. Budgeting for the events you repeat will be done with reference to previous years, and then adding your estimate of any likely increases in expenditure and income. (Bear in mind any rate of inflation agreed with your finance officer and/or treasurer.) For a new event it will be much more difficult and it is advisable to be conservative.

Example: budgeting for a concert

If you are going to organise, say, a concert, then you will need to look at all aspects of possible expenditure and find a way of estimating the income. The best starting point is to borrow someone else's knowledge and particularly their experience. You will find that most experienced fundraisers will give you quite a lot of information if they have a few minutes free.

- Talk to other fundraisers about their events. Ask about their successes and failures. (This applies, of course, not just to income and expenditure, but also to management of the event.)

- For an event where you are expecting to make money from those taking part, the key is to estimate how many will attend and how much they will give on average. Concert-goers will be attending because they wish to see and hear the star. They will not go and sit through a performance they cannot stand because they wish to support your organisation. So, the previous pulling power of the entertainer will be your guide to the size of venue you can book and the amount to charge.

- You will also need nerves of steel when it comes to deciding whether the artist or artists that do say yes can really fit the bill and fill the hall. Again, people will be paying because they think the event is value for money, not in order to give you extra funds. They will also naively believe that everything is free to you, including the hall, orchestra, publicity, sound system, after-show party (very important for your key donors and for thanking the celebrities), etc. So you must ascertain how much people usually pay to attend your celebrities' events or this kind of performance. That will give you the greater part of your income.

- You should also make money from advertisements in the programme. Ask all the tradespeople who supply you with the goods your organisation uses during the year to buy space in the brochure, and do not forget to invite them to the after-show party.

- Valuable extra funds can come from such things as a bucket collection afterwards and T-shirt sales. If you are fortunate enough you will actually make more money from sales of 'product' ie. video, TV film, cassettes, etc., than from the event. But unless contracts are signed, do not budget for income from that source, as it is notoriously unreliable.

- Having calculated the income, deduct between 10% and 20% for publicity (posters, adverts, etc.). Be ready to write and phone the media relentlessly to obtain as much editorial coverage as possible and as many listings as you can.

- Find out how much you need to pay for the hall, how much to fly in your stars and meet their other transport and hotel expenses. (Their management will have a standard list of outrageous demands to be met.)

- Think carefully about the cost of the sound system, stage decoration, rehearsals (hall rental and professional musician costs), the production manager, etc. Be exhaustive in thinking through all the stages of running the show, because extra costs traditionally eat up much more than the expected profits on concerts.

- If, at the end of all this, you can still estimate a profit, check the break-even point, that is, how many tickets you need to sell to get your money back. If you can do this on half the sales and still make a healthy profit if only two-thirds of the tickets sell, then you have an event worth running. In practice the margins may be tighter than this and you will need to make a professional judgement (taking as much experienced expert advice as possible) on whether or not to proceed.

Key to success

The actual figures you use should always be conservative. The rule is that your expenditure always happens and the organisation always spends any income you estimate will arrive - so you had better be sure it does!

Be very tough in resisting pressure to pad out your estimated income so that someone's favourite project can be funded. You will not be thanked later when the expected income does not materialise and the organisation cuts expenditure in the most vulnerable areas, which often means staff costs.

The budget line, then, will simply show the expected income and expenditure for the planned event. If you expect to convert a significant number of people into members as a result of that event, then the consequent income should appear in a membership development line, (not just in the membership subscriptions line), and credited to the event during its evaluation.

Planning

Integrating planning and budgeting

Your master plan can be quite simple; just a sheet of A4 paper with the months of the year across the top, the list of planned fundraising activities down the left-hand side, and a series of crosses in the squares under the months where you plan these activities.(See Fig 1b.)

It is very useful to indicate on the plan any other activities scheduled by the rest of your organisation that may affect your plans. For example, the dates

PLANNED FUNDRAISING ACTIVITIES								
	Jan	Feb	Mar	Apr	May	Jun	July	etc.
Advertisements	●		●		●		●	
Direct mail		●		●		●		
Magazine inserts	●			●			●	
Newsletter	●			●			●	
Appeals		●			●			●
Concerts				●				
Art auctions		●						
Etc.								

Fig. 1b *A simple plan of the year's fundraising.*

when any newsletters are issued are important, because you will schedule your appeals to members at suitable intervals between them in such a way as to avoid members feeling that you could have placed your appeal in the newsletter and saved the postage. (The popular press has trained the public to be eagle-eyed about unnecessary expenditure by charities, and to retain their confidence you should be one step ahead.) Incidentally, if you were to place your appeal in the newsletter the sharp fall in response would far outweigh the saving in postage. (Or would it? If you are not sure, test!)

Naturally, you will also need to work out exactly who is going to undertake each of these activities, when they should start, and the key stages at which you will need to monitor progress. Don't try to do everything yourself.

For the purposes of budgeting you need to be certain that each of these activities really will take place. This is not a wish list. The organisation is about to set out how it will spend the profit from these activities, and it will be your responsibility to see that they occur at the level of profit you say will be generated. Be conservative, but do not simply underestimate to give yourself an easy time. Be prudent, but not pessimistic. Your treasurer should rein in your natural optimism.

Income projections

- For each activity you plan, calculate the expenditure and the income:
  - each category, e.g. advertising, loose-leaf inserts, trading, will probably form a separate budget line.
  - each event will have its own line.
- Before you begin work on the budget, the organisation's financial advisers (usually the treasurer, head of finance and director) will set the basic budget parameters with you. These include the organisation's estimate for inflation

next year, the cost of borrowing, etc. The parameters should be conservative, and may give one rate for the increase in prices you will face and another for the percentage increase in donations (the estimated increase in costs possibly being higher than that in income).

- A view should be taken on the effect of any increase in membership or subscription fees. Unless this is dramatic it will have no effect on the overall numbers recruited by any particular means, as the membership fees of most organisations are far less than the average donation - which is a clear indication they are far too low. Many organisations receive, on average, a donation of one third of the fee on top of their membership income. This shows that members themselves recognise that their fee is too low to be properly effective. You may, of course, experience difficulty in convincing your board or council of this.

- For each of your projected activities use historical data from previous years to check for any trends. Increase expenditure by cost inflation, and income by the agreed amount, and you will begin to build up a picture of the financial future.

- Calculate at an early stage the increase in the number of members or donors. This is especially important, as it will affect many of the other budget lines, setting the amount of income from appeals, raffles, trading, and any other activity dependent on membership numbers. For those activities it is essential to multiply the average cost and income (adjusted as before) by the average number of expected members and/or donors in the new financial year. This is where the effect of past and future investment is felt. If you have had the foresight to invest strongly in membership/donor development you will see a correspondingly rapid growth in your income.

- The next area to work out is the expenditure on membership/donor acquisition. This is the key to your future income. Unless your organisation is very popular, this expenditure will be in the form of an investment whereby you lose money in the first year but come into a very healthy profit in year two and each following year for the whole of the member's or donor's 'life' with you. (A slight dip in income as donors retire is usually outweighed by legacy income as your planned giving programme takes effect. Students often leave the organisation in the early years of their career, but return later if the organisation is still relevant and dynamic.)

The next three years and beyond

The interaction of planning and budgeting

In any one year it is likely that the organisation will have far more activities that it wishes to undertake than it can afford to fund, and it is easy to succumb to the temptation to reduce investment in fundraising. Only when the draft budgets for future years make it clear that this would drastically reduce future income, and therefore future programme activity, can the temptation be successfully resisted, and your expenditure budget increased by an amount which will ensure adequate growth for the organisation.

It is therefore important for you, along with the organisation's key financial advisers, to plan the draft budgets for a number of years so that the organisation can make a sound decision about investment. This is usually an iterative and time-consuming process, which involves going backwards and forwards, checking what will happen in two or three years time for such and such a level of investment. Putting your calculations on a spreadsheet could save your sanity.

To do this accurately it is essential to know how long members and donors stay with your organisation (on average), from each of the different areas of recruitment, and how much they give in additional income. This will both guide the amount of loss you can afford to bear in year one (the more the income over lifetime, the greater the loss that can be borne), and indicate the optimum areas for investment.

Key to success

It would be rash to invest in just the most profitable one or two areas, because the business cycle operates as inexorably with charities as it does with any other commercial activity, and you may experience, for example, a slowing down of the response to direct mail, and an improvement in advertising revenue. It is tempting to think this makes nonsense of budget estimates - but these are not accurate predictions of what will happen, just the best estimates given the current state of knowledge.

Naturally, you will take corrective action if things change for the worse, and take advantage if they improve. You will need a degree of flexibility to spend extra money when things go very well (roll-over income). If this is not in the budget you may need to go back to your director, treasurer or finance subcommittee, so this possibility should be discussed during the budget process.

This overall process should be used to plan the next few years' investment in fundraising and subsequent income generation. Whether the organisation can really afford all this investment will be revealed by the balance sheet and the Hon. Treasurer's view of the necessary level of reserves and the cash flow situation.

Planning your cash flow

As part of your planning it is important to know when the organisation may become short of money and how soon this will be made up by future income flows. This will allow funds to be borrowed and repaid on time or an overdraft to be arranged.

When you have mapped out the income and expenditure necessary for each activity in the year, it is easy to total this up month by month. Bear in mind:

* the time taken to receive and pay bills

- the time taken for income to arrive
  - newspaper advertising revenue will mostly come in during the following week or two
  - direct mail revenue will come in the following month
  - revenue from loose-leaf inserts will come in during the following two months
  - appeals to the donor-base will take a few weeks
  - anything with a monthly giving form will naturally be in twelve monthly instalments.

Ask your head of administration and finance how long it really takes before the tax is reclaimed on covenants, etc. Double that in your calculations.

This cash flow, when compared with the flow of expenditure, will reveal the months when you may need to borrow from the bank or dip into reserves. If you do not need to do this you are probably being far too cautious in your investment in fundraising.

Tax efficient donations

Throughout this book tax efficient donations will be mentioned in several places. A donation made to a registered charity can be simply sent by cheque or put into a collecting box. However, if your donors can be encouraged to give tax effectively, your charity can claim back the tax from the Inland Revenue. In some cases those paying tax at the higher rate can claim back, for themselves, the difference between the standard rate (which the charity will reclaim) and the higher rate. Of course, you have to be a tax payer for these schemes to work.

The methods of giving which offer this possibility have been progressively extended in recent years and both the lowest payment threshold and the ceiling for such payments shifted to assist charities.

The principal methods of tax effective giving are Gift Aid, Covenants, Payroll Giving, Legacies, and where capital gains tax has been incurred on the sale of assets and through the Charities Aid Foundation scheme.

Gift aid

You can make a tax effective donation of £250 or more to any charity via a gift aid form (R190 SD for individuals, R240 SD for companies) . The charity can claim back the tax already paid and higher rate tax payers can claim back (on their tax returns) the additional 15% they have paid. A £750 donation would then be worth £1,000 to the recipient.

Covenants

A deed of covenant is a promise to pay a certain amount annually for at least four years for no material consideration (ie. it must be a true gift and as a rule of thumb any incentive, eg. newsletter, received in return should be worth less than 2.5% of the gift). Covenants must be made out on an appropriate form - the deed, which, incidentally, does not need an expiry date. N.B. If the forms are to be used in Scotland they will need to be slightly different. Again higher rate tax payers can reclaim the extra 15% they have paid.

Payroll giving

Many companies employ substantial numbers of workers and many professional groups, like legal practices, now run such schemes. The money is deducted via the payroll before tax is taken out and passed to a charity agency (of which there are several, though Give As You Earn run by CAF is probably the best known) which then passes the funds on according to your request. Companies often select a small group of charities to benefit from their schemes. The maximum amount that you can give has recently been raised to £1,200.

Legacies

Gifts to charity from your estate are free of inheritance tax.

Capital gains

This is a useful way of avoiding tax and not passing on the burden. Suppose you have £1000 worth of shares that would incur capital gains tax if they were sold. You can give them to a charity without incurring the capital gains tax yourself and not passing that tax burden on to the charity.

CAF

The Charities Aid Foundation run an ingenious scheme for those donors who wish to make occasional payments to different charities tax effectively. The donor makes tax-efficient payments to CAF and they issue a 'cheque book' from which cheques can be sent to any charity.

International budgeting

Many charities or not-for-profit organisations have a loose international network of sister organisations. Occasionally, these contribute to the centre a percentage of their income, or even all their profits. Often they receive money from the centre to fund their charitable or campaigning activities. Equally often the centre does very little to assist the overseas divisions, though the more dynamic multinationals are beginning to invest heavily in the former second and third world countries. This investment is yielding rich rewards as tried and tested techniques are used on their large, affluent caring classes with little or no competition.

Budgeting for this is difficult the first time around, and it is best to set up an investment fund to be spent in each country whose market you wish to penetrate, rather than budgeting for an early return. The usual careful monitoring will reveal what has gone right and where improvements are needed, which will lead to proper estimates in subsequent years. The returns can be so large that it is tempting to keep ploughing back the profits and go for growth while you are alone in the market - but do not forget that your organisation's public profile and respect for your work are vital factors in fundraising and need to keep pace with your financial investment.

Overseas strategy

A common error is for large charities to consider their separate operations or overseas branches as financially distinct from each other, to the extent that although they would like, say, the hospice side of their programme to grow much more rapidly, they will simply not consider using funds available in another sector as seedcorn to accelerate the process. This is particularly noticeable in the case of overseas branches. It may have taken the American parent charity forty years to reach its current size but they will puzzle over why the Brazilian branch is taking so long to grow, without giving it any of the experience or funds it needs to improve its income.

Even more serious and prevalent is the mind-set that sees any overseas operation in terms of 'that's where we spend the money we raise over here'. Having invested a large amount of time in ensuring that 85% of all the funds raised go to projects overseas, it is hard to realise that this involves a false distinction: if a reasonable investment of both experience and money were made in fundraising in any country in the world, some funds could be efficiently raised to supplement or replace the grants currently made.

It may also be more effective in the long term to spend a higher proportion of available funds on fundraising overseas to give greater growth. Multi-national companies are beginning to operate in this way, and are becoming multi-domestics (manufacturing and selling in several different countries) with a much greater international spread of all their operations, or global companies having the head office in one country, manufacturing in several and sales in, say, Asia, the USA and Europe. For those organisations that would like their overseas branches to expand, the current pattern is often as if Henry Ford, having decided Spain was a good place to make and sell Ford cars, had set up a bicycle works there and waited for it to grow into a fully integrated factory.

Of course, the kind of development I'm advocating would alter the earlier equation and complicate the issue of how much is spent on overheads - which has always been a relatively false consideration for many organisations, as their programme work is often mainly overheads by its nature. The overseas development agencies have had a simple answer to criticism of such overhead expenditure, because they could point to the amount going overseas compared with the amount spent in the home country. However, this defence is not available to many organisations which have the onerous task of explaining the nature of their expenditure to an often sceptical and ill-informed audience.

Fundraising reports

You cannot possibly budget, counter changing market conditions, or take full advantage of good fortune if you do not have prompt feedback on how your work is going. Unfortunately, for most finance departments (apart from a few enlightened individuals), letting you know the returns on your work is far from their minds. You will probably need to run the department which receives the cheques, as well as the membership department which controls the donor-base - otherwise the time-lag in learning what has happened may be crippling.

In an organisation of, say, 100,000 members with a turnover of £10m principally from those members, the core reports you will need are:

- a weekly report by source code, giving you the number of members, the number of donors and amount of income from each source, such as direct mail, loose-leaf inserts, etc.
- a similar daily report for each advertising code.
- a weekly report for each event (raffles, street collections, concerts, etc.), indicating the number of people giving and the amount received.
- a weekly report of unsolicited donations: number and amount.
- a weekly report of appeals income (number and amount of donations). This will be more sophisticated if you segment your appeals.
- reports on the sale of merchandise. This is both the amount of sales and number of purchases, but also information on individual sales for stock control purposes. (See Chapter 5.)

In addition to these reports you will need to know:

- if your organisation has a non-charitable as well as a charitable wing, how each is performing as a distinct entity.
- by what method people are giving (for example, if a membership drive has brought in the fees in cash only it will not be as valuable as if they are all in direct debits).
- membership by type of member (e.g., single, student, family, platinum, gold, silver, etc.). Lapse rates for each category would also be useful.

This is a far from exhaustive list, but anything less will put a brake on your efforts and adversely affect your organisation's income.

Setting up a department

Departments are rarely, if ever, planned. Usually they just grow as the pressure of work overwhelms individuals or the champions and pioneers of various kinds of fundraising have their way in demanding resources for their particular projects.

Starting from scratch

Setting up a department from scratch is the ideal situation, but few of us will ever be that fortunate. The first posts to be established should be those that build the base of the fundraising pyramid, then those that deal with its further development. Later the trading and company posts will emerge, depending on the type of interest that the organisation commands.

Obviously, the basic characteristics of your organisation will influence the development of the fundraising department. The National Trust has excellent properties across the country which can house shops that cater for their visitors. Barnardo's has a very experienced legacy department. Oxfam has grown historically through its charity shops. All these organisations, have the usual range of fundraising employees, but also need specialist staff.

Some organisations will have the government or trusts as their principal source of revenue and this will also require specialist staff. However, such sources do tend by their nature to be rather uncertain providers of long-term finance.

The fundraising department should be linked organically with the rest of the organisation and not be considered a very separate or different part. This helps fundraising to serve the organisation's core aims and objectives as well as raising money. Usually the best fundraising has a strong element or programme of advocacy in it, and can be a powerful tool for advancing the organisation's goals.

Planning growth

A planned approach to growth will enable your organisation to anticipate the resources needed ahead of your request, and to budget for that need in advance. If things are working out well, and it becomes necessary to have additional staff or space or computer equipment, it is far easier to acquire the resource if you have made people aware of the reasons for your request ahead of time, so that they can consider it before being faced with the actual decision.

Planning also allows you to develop those areas of income generation that will maximise the overall income rather than those that may just be someone's pet project. Not planning growth can lead to huge gaps between potential income and performance as well as a very poor staff income ratio.

You must be careful to consider:

- the profile of the organisation. A high profile is essential for effective fundraising but it may come from an area of fundraising that is not particularly profitable such as advertising or national events. These, then, must be encouraged, not dropped on performance grounds alone. It is usual, however, for a fundraising action which brings a high profile to be very profitable. Profiles rise and fall and a time of high profile is usually a good time to increase investment in membership/donor recruitment.

- in any fundraising department there should be several activities or events which are in the process of being developed into major income earners, but which are not yet very profitable.

Planning events

Typically, it takes three years for an event to mature.

- In the first year you will make many mistakes and probably a loss.

- In the second year you can expect a profit, provided you have analysed your mistakes and acted to correct them, as your expertise grows and begins to take effect. You will find out the best pricing policy, the right size and location of venue, the best time of year, etc. Your audience will return and bring their friends, and the stars who give their time for free will know you are capable of putting on a good show, making it easier to recruit their friends and for them to return.

- In the third year all this should all come together to give a large profit; and in subsequent years it can grow until its time passes and a new kind of event is needed to replace it. In this context an event could be the opening of a shop chain, beginning a legacy campaign, starting regional fundraising, etc.

Staffing

   The size and shape of a fundraising department varies with the availability of volunteers and the use of consultants. With a freely available supply of volunteers and lots of consultants the actual staffing can be quite low. With all fundraising work done by in-house staff the department can be much larger especially if income processing and recording is also undertaken.

§

Of course, you can fundraise without having a strategy, or planning or budgeting, in the same way as you can journey up the Amazon without consulting a map or buying provisions, but your chances of returning successfully from your venture are immeasurably increased if you think ahead. We have a duty to exercise what the Quakers call 'good husbandry' over our organisation's resources and this cannot be done without an appropriate strategy.

The following chapters look in detail at the techniques that could be combined into such a strategy and at other relevant issues. Because the bulk of charitable giving comes from individual donations rather than companies or governments this is addressed first.

2 The Fundraising Pyramid

The Pareto principle

The fundraising pyramid, aided and abetted by the Pareto principle, has been the fundraising professional's touchstone for many years now. Pareto was a polymath and, among other professions, a psychologist, who observed that in any group of organisms, 80% of activity came from only 20% of them. Marketing experts use the same principle, knowing that in general they can obtain 80% of their orders from 20% of their customers.

Once fundraisers had considered the Pareto principle in relation to maximising income from an organisation's supporters, the information technology revolution had provided helpful computers with infinite storage and recall systems, and American direct mail gurus had tested every possible variation in appeal letters, there was little to do but sit back and let the money roll in. The majority of successful non-governmental organisations (NGOs) in North America, Europe and Australasia now pursue a fundraising strategy based on the Pareto principle and refined by the common experience of countless NGOs, from Church groups to pressure groups, and from hospitals to political parties.

The central tenet of the strategy is to build up those areas of fundraising that maximise income in the medium to long term, ie. , three to five years, the timescale best suited to maximising returns from investment in a donor-base. The key elements in this process are illustrated in Fig. 2a. Of course, any areas of fundraising that look promising in the short term are not neglected; you need to vary the mix of fundraising techniques as a defence against the effects of the product cycle.

At each step up the pyramid the numbers giving decline, but the amount given increases, and it is only with extensive work at the top levels that the 80/20 ratio can be met.

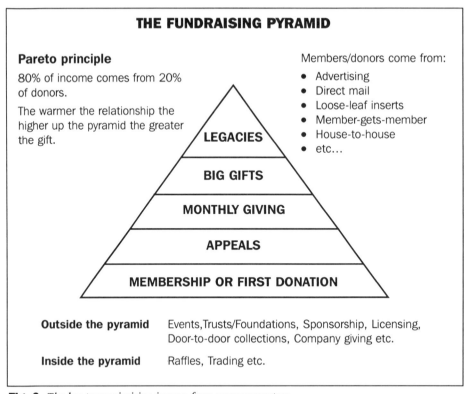

Fig. 2 *The key to maximising income from your supporters.*

The five levels of the pyramid

The base of the pyramid

The base of the pyramid consists of supporters who have made an initial donation or paid their first subscription. They are not, however, really supporters until they have made their second donation or renewed their subscription, as their initial gift may have been just a passing whim, spurred by an effective piece of fundraising. Fortunately, however, the trend among donors is away from impulsive giving and towards making deliberate choices of organisation, to which they remain committed, but only if they find the organisation effective in fulfilling their expectations.

Translating that initial gift into a lifetime's support is therefore crucial, and starts with the organisation's first contact with the donor. This should make them feel good about their gift, that it is appreciated, and will make a difference. It should be a positive experience, warm and timely, the start of a long-term relationship: at this point the donor has the highest regard for the organisation, and is very open to suggestions about how to help in future. Many organisations waste this opportunity by sending the annual report, the latest newsletter, any leaflet that comes easily to hand, and a photocopied letter from the director that has not had its date changed for a few decades.

- The first communication should be one of thanks. From the code on the membership form returned by the supporter, you should know if joining or donating is in reply to an advertisement, a loose-leaf insert, or whatever, and the theme and content of the appeal. The letter should mention this: 'Thank you for responding to our recent advertisement concerning ...'.

- If your real need is to develop monthly giving, this is the best time to emphasise and encourage it. Rarely will the donor be as receptive again.

- Set out all the possible options for donors to help you (financially and otherwise), and allow them to choose simply, say, by ticking the appropriate box and returning the form in a reply-paid envelope. It is a good idea to use a brief questionnaire to learn more about your new friends.

- Make sure that you do not put the organisation between the donor and the person they are trying to help. People give to people, not organisations.

The results of split-testing direct mail letters (dividing the mailing list into at least two distinct parts with different codes on each reply device, so that the difference in pulling power between the variations in the pack can be accurately evaluated) indicate that recipients of direct mail letters tend to be very hesitant. They are by nature very shy, need clear, strong guidance about how to respond, and will not act at all if given the least cause for concern.

In practice this means that if someone has to look for a stamp, write out their name and address, or buy an envelope, they are far less likely to reply. Hence it pays to make things really easy.

Keys to success

- Offer a form with the donor's name and address clearly printed on it, so that they have very little to fill in, preferably just tick-boxes stating how much they are giving.

- Supply a FREEPOST or pre-paid envelope to return the form in.

- Make matters easier for yourself by using window envelopes in conjunction with the address on the reply form, thus avoiding the need to match two labels in the same pack.

Legal note: the Data Protection Act

Under the Data Protection Act, if you intend to hold names and addresses on computer, then you should let people know this clearly at the point of joining, if you intend to use these for any purpose supporters would not normally associate with membership or the reason why they responded. The information must be as clearly presented as all other information. According to the Data Protection Register's particular view, this does not include reciprocal mailings from other organisations. These are classified as trading, not direct mail . You must register such activity as trading. You have been warned! (See Chapter 9.)

It is a wise precaution to include this information in the new members' pack as well, mentioning that people can opt out if they wish. Many organisations are now often mentioning reciprocals in their advertising and other first-point-of-contact literature.

The second level of the pyramid

On the second level of the pyramid are donors who have responded to an appeal. (Usually this will have been a direct mail appeal.) Ways of soliciting donations, in descending order of effectiveness, are:

- face-to-face
- telephone call
- personal letter
- impersonal circular.

This order reflects the fact that these methods are progressively more personal and more interactive. The last two methods allow questions about the organisation to be answered immediately.

The most cost-effective approach for donor-bases in the tens or hundreds of thousands is usually direct mail letter. A number of these can be sent each year, provided they have a genuine and persuasive reason for requesting that extra donation.

Test to ascertain the point at which an increase in the number of appeals becomes counter-productive. The maximum appears to be twelve per year, largely because most people are paid twelve times in the year, but many organisations limit their appeals to a maximum of six per year, for logistical reasons and because, when appeals have arrived within a month of each other, the results have been far worse than expected. Most organisations seem to average four per year.

Newsletters

In between these appeals members usually receive a newsletter. This serves a very important function for the organisation. The newsletter is the key mechanism whereby your relationship with your supporters is built up and developed. It should

- educate readers regarding the nature of the organisation they have joined, its objectives, how these are achieved, and how effective and efficient the organisation is in achieving them.
- show clearly that the cause is worth supporting, ie. that a very serious problem exists and that the organisation is addressing it effectively.

Through reading the newsletter the supporter should become more knowledgeable about the organisation in a way that leads to a long-term commitment. There is no reason why the supporter should not also be led to become a campaigning activist as well as an active donor, e.g. by writing letters or joining a local group; but the prime purpose of a national membership or donor-base is to secure the financial future of an organisation.

Showing appreciation

The psychology of activists (and staff and volunteers) is very different to that of donors. Activists basically give time, and donors mainly give money. Neither should be made to feel guilty about this, or that their contribution is in some way second best.

Activists are usually brought together in local groups for mutual support. Donating, on the other hand, is often a lone or perhaps a family event. Acknowledgement of this act is the key to its repetition. The thank-you letter (or phone call) should be prompt, apt and friendly, letting recipients know that the organisation has appreciated their personal generosity and will use the money in the way that was intended, and to good effect.

During their lifetime a person may, however, change from being a student activist to, say, being a young donor, then a local group activist, then a top donor and later leave a legacy, so make sure your supporters realise you welcome these changes.

The third level of the pyramid

The third level of the pyramid is populated by those who have arranged with their bank to make a regular (usually monthly) donation to the organisation, as well as paying their subscription. Often the inducement for this method of giving is a donor club whose subscription is much larger than the usual fee. In return, club members receive special privileges.

Many organisations have several of these clubs with different levels of giving: for example, the WWF has Gold, Silver and Bronze members. American zoos have the Chairman's, Keepers' and Friends' Clubs. Often club members pay substantial fees. This system is possible, firstly, because people are usually paid monthly, and a relatively small monthly donation is much easier than the same sum taken from one month's pay; and, secondly, because the clubs are formed to meet the needs of donors at higher levels of giving.

Often, monthly givers are not approached again with regular appeals. (Sometimes this is used as an inducement to become a monthly giver.) This is a mistake, however, as donors soon miss the involvement of helping by responding to appeals, and receiving their regular thank-you letters, and begin donating again. Many donors cannot even remember to which organisations their standing orders or covenants are made out. Often they donate to show approval of a particular project, and miss that close involvement with the work of the organisation when they become monthly givers and the opportunity represented by appeals is taken away. Club members are usually among the highest givers to appeals.

Amnesty International in the UK has a club, the 'Partners of Conscience' scheme, whereby members make out a covenant for at least £5 per month. Under UK law a covenant allows Amnesty to collect from the government the tax paid by donors on their gifts. Club members receive a smart but discreet lapel pin in gold and black, bearing Amnesty's logo and the club name.

Segment your donors into groups by dividing them up on the basis of their previous gifts (in total, per annum and by the largest amount given at one time). This analysis should reveal how many clear categories they fall into, and so how many clubs you could create, and the level of giving and rewards appropriate to each club. This will usually be a rather messy value judgement, and should involve a testing programme to ascertain what level of annual or monthly gift people are happy with, and which rewards meet their own needs best. These can be needs for recognition, thanks, a feeling of armchair involvement, actual hands-on experience of the work, confirmation of status or real improvement in social status, the opportunity to meet celebrities, etc. It is usually worthwhile to test your ideas by discussing them with small groups of supporters, being very careful not to lead them to tell you just what you want to hear.

Covenants

Covenants are a promise to pay a stipulated amount for at least four years for no material consideration, ie. any return to the donor is of very little value. It is worth checking the assumed worth of your newsletter or other club benefits with your VAT inspector. The covenant can, however, run on for the donor's lifetime, so it is not wise to put a finishing date on the covenant form.

Covenants can only be made out to a registered charity, which can then reclaim the tax already paid on sums donated. The Charities Aid Foundation runs an excellent scheme, administering covenants and collecting the tax for those charities which find this an administrative burden - even many quite large charities become hopelessly behind in reclaiming their tax.

Linking the covenant to a direct debit is sensible, as the bank administration of banker's orders has become a nightmare. In much of Europe this will take the form of an auto giro payment. Check a variety of other organisations' literature to see how covenants are best made out stylistically but always take legal advice on the final form and remember the law is different in Scotland.

The fourth level of the pyramid

The next level of the pyramid is drawn from those who make a special, major gift to the organisation. Usually, these people are researched, located and systematically approached to support special projects requiring large donations. This could be in relation to a capital appeal (say, for a new building) or for an important new area of work, etc. The solicitation can be done in one of several ways.

Research

Potential major donors are often members of monthly giving clubs, and many organisations do very well merely by creating separate clubs for their top donors which have very high entrance fees and suitable incentives. Often major donors can be found by comparing your donor-base with lists of affluent individuals. The best fundraising consultancies should be able to do this for you electronically. The third key route to discovering major donors is by encouraging your known major donors and influential supporters to use their networks to produce prospects for you.

The approach

The best approach is always face-to-face, whether you are raising a few hundred pounds for a playgroup or a few million for a new University building. The approach should be made by someone in the same peer group as the potential donor, preferably someone who is known to them and who has given themselves.

Whether the approach is through a personal visit or by phone, letter or email, a persuasive case needs to be developed beforehand, and presented along with a clear statement of the amount being asked for.

The potential

Big gift clubs and individual solicitations to major donors are key techniques in the fundraiser's repertoire. The Pareto principle shows just how important they can be for your organisation. They are more fully explored in Chapter 4 in the 'Monthly giving' and 'Big gift appeals' sections.

The apex of the pyramid

Finally, at the apex of the donor pyramid, sits the legacy or bequest programme or, as it is increasingly called, the 'planned giving' programme.

A bequest leaving a percentage of the estate is often called a residuary legacy. There are also pecuniary legacies where a sum of money is left, and specific bequests where an object is left. Always let people know that a valuable object is quite acceptable. Many charities have been left valuable oil paintings, china collections and even houses! Reversionary or life interest wills are those that take care of friends or family by giving them a stated interest in the estate. A member of the family might, for example, be allowed to live in the house during their lifetime, which would afterwards revert to the charity. This is a useful way of securing the interests of the family and still ensuring that a charity benefits.

Sources of legacies

Legacies appear to come from two sources. One source is people who have never made a donation to the organisation and do not appear anywhere in the records; and the other is people who have given regularly through a large part of their lifetime and continue that practice by planning their future and final gift. Interestingly, legacies come equally from both sources.

This means that you should take a broad approach.

• Remind all supporters that it is possible to leave money or goods to the organisation in their will (and, if it is a charity, that it can be done most tax-effectively), after they have taken care of their families.

• Those who are not known supporters also need to be reached. The main method of doing this is to advertise a free will-making guide in the press and, naturally, to introduce the organisation in that guide. (Your donors' research questionnaire will tell you which newspapers and magazines your supporters read.) It is customary, in doing this, to ask the recipient to let the organisation know if they are leaving a legacy to it, offering an incentive to do so in the form of a small but suitable gift such as a pen, badge or book, or putting their name in a remembrance book. A remembrance book may seem a quaint idea but if you are leaving money in your will the thought that your generosity will be recorded permanently is very powerful.

Incentives

Generally, incentives work well and are a useful tool for the fundraiser. In many areas of fundraising, from appeals to the returning of lifestyle questionnaires, the introduction of incentives yields an improved response.

If you use incentives they should be

• appropriate to the organisation. (For example, Amnesty sometimes uses a pen as an incentive because it calls on its members to write letters, and Friends of the Earth will plant a tree in the name of someone leaving a legacy.)

• of good quality, because, to the donor, they reflect the quality of the organisation's work.

• accompanied, when used in an appeal, by a clear indication of the level of giving you would like to see, so that the donor feels comfortable at that level, rather than worrying about being thought foolish for giving so much or mean for giving so little.

In Amnesty's loose-leaf inserts a good quality fountain pen was offered to people who gave £35 or more. Split tests showed that this led to a rise in the number of people giving £35, and an even bigger rise in the number who gave £50. The perceived value of the pens was, of course, much higher than their actual cost, and the increase in income was at least five times greater than the added cost.

The psychology behind incentives used in this way is that they give reassurance, rather than a reason to give. If you give donors an incentive to return a coupon which indicates planned giving, they receive a message that the organisation regards this as an important way of helping. They respond to that message, rather than simply acting to gain the incentive.

Visiting solicitors and bank managers

The other main method of encouraging legacies is to organise a volunteer team to visit solicitors and bank managers, letting them know all about the organisation and leaving posters and leaflets for them to use if asked to advise on an appropriate organisation. Though solicitors will not put forward any particular organisation without being asked, they are often called on to suggest names of organisations in certain categories.

Advertising in the *Law Society Gazette* or *Solicitors' Journal* serves a similar purpose, as these are the two main publications shown to clients from which to pick a charity. There is no research to suggest how effective the plethora of other publications might be. (See also Legacy Leaflets and Advocacy, Chapter 4.)

Befriending elderly supporters

In recent years a new approach has grown up which is very close to a much needed social work programme for the elderly. This works extraordinarily well and will become a very large component of most voluntary sector organisations' fundraising, though it is still in its infancy at the moment.

The approach is for a full-time member of staff to identify those people who are both elderly and major supporters of the organisation, and to return to them some of the kindness they have shown during their lives to the organisation. This can range from the occasional call, to spending time with the donor, to carrying out errands and assisting with difficulties. This is always at the donor's complete discretion, and does not involve any approach for funds. This service is often very highly valued by the elderly.

Other techniques for use inside the pyramid

There are several other fairly significant ways of drawing funds from supporters in the pyramid. The most important of these for many organisations are raffles which are covered in Chapter 4.

Another key area is trading. Supporters provide a sympathetic niche market and will buy branded goods at a premium. This operation can also be used to provide a springboard for selling outside the pyramid to the general public through licensing deals, the stocking of branded goods in shops and on-pack promotion. Trading is covered thoroughly in Chapter 5.

§

The fundraising pyramid is now a traditional tool but one which has been improved by good practice over the years. Relationship fundraising has codified much of this improvement though how closely our fundraising can match with all our donors' needs and still remain efficient has yet to be determined.

What is certain is that for any organisation that can raise large numbers of supporters the pyramid provides a simple framework for effectively maximising the income from those supporters over a number of years.

3 Building the Pyramid: Recruiting Members and Donors

Advertising

The best thing about advertising is that it makes your current supporters feel good about their support and introduces thousands of people to your work, who, although they may not give now, will give when they have been asked a few more times. Most people joining or giving through newspaper advertising say that they had intended to give for some time before seeing the advertisement that finally triggered their action.

You are fortunate if you have an advertising budget large enough to warrant employing an advertising agency. Even so, the chances are that you will need to guide your agency carefully in the tough world of charity advertising. Unfortunately, most charities do not have a extensive series of shops across the country where their products can be bought, and so advertising agencies cannot use their usual techniques to help. If you only have a small budget, you will need to weigh the costs and benefits of using an advertising agency very carefully.

The secret of charity advertising

The secret of advertising for charities is to prevent your advertising agency from trying to enhance your profile or engage in prestige advertising, but to have them treat the advertisement just like a piece of direct mail which requires an immediate response.

An excellent book on advertising is *Ogilvy on Advertising* by David Ogilvy, who founded the giant advertising agency Ogilvy and Mather. It was published by Guild Publishing in 1985, but I doubt if it is still in print. If you see it, buy it!

Commercial advertising and charity advertising: the crucial difference

Good commercial advertising works long after the advertisement has been seen. It makes sure that when the customer is looking for a product he or she has a favourable impression of the company's brand firmly in mind at decision-making time. It takes a long time (and often much money) to establish this. The advertiser will know what benefits the customer is likely to require from the product - customers are purchasing the benefits of the product not the product itself - and which newspapers, journals and TV spots the customer is likely to watch. This will be established through thorough research. You can use similar techniques to discover where it is best to advertise for new supporters, and who are the most likely kinds of people to support your cause.

The crucial difference is, however, that your supporters will be required to respond immediately by filling in a coupon and posting it with their cheque to your organisation. This means that they must stop their perusal of the paper and feel so strongly that something must be done about your cause that they will fill out the coupon there and then.

The way to do this is to create a powerful headline to hold their interest and a dramatic picture that tells a significant part of the story, with just enough text to bring them to the most important part - the coupon.

The Advertisement

The headline

The headline is often much harder than the rest of the text for an agency copywriter to compose, because they are trained to write a line which tells the story and sticks in your mind for a long while afterwards. This is often done with an intellectual twist, such as a pun or play on words. If the story is told in the headline the reader will 'get the picture' and move on. A good charity headline impels the reader, if he or she has a heart, to read the rest of the text and then to respond. This is not easy for copywriters trained to write commercial advertisements. The headline must be physically large and bold to stand out above the other headlines on the page.

The text

The text can be quite long (but need not be the full page format which Amnesty has found successful). A succinct statement of the problem, and why joining or giving money will help to solve it, is all that is really needed for most organisations. A large amount of text requires a brilliant copywriter who makes it well worthwhile for the reader to read every word. If one paragraph is boring, unnecessary or irritating, the reader will turn over the page.

Judging advertising copy

Most advertising copy will be short, as the advertisements will only occupy a small space on the page. Legibility is the first requirement. Do not be tempted to cram a large amount of copy, however well written, into such a small space that it is hard to read. People just will not bother to read it and will turn the page. Be ruthless with your copywriter in this regard. Do not reverse out your text,

Brazil has solved the problem of how to keep kids off the streets. Kill them.

Street children who have no-one to look after them help one another. More than one child every day is killed by police death squads.

When Brazilian street children have nightmares, they are not necessarily dreaming.

7,000,000 children live rough in Brazil, some in flimsy shanties, others in city sewers.

They have learned to fear the car that pulls up at night from which heavily armed men jump out. The sound of police boots clattering through the sewers.

The screams as children are caught, the cries and sobs as they are beaten and the flat, final crack of gunshots.

This sounds incredible, but it's true.

Children's corpses, often bearing marks of torture, are turning up at the rate of more than one a day in the streets of Brazil.

A recent study by the Brazilian Institute for Social and Economic Analysis reported that 457 children or adolescents were killed by death squads in just three cities last year.

It came to the conclusion that the squads, many of them run by off-duty policemen, kill "to clean up the streets."

Nor is Brazil the only country in which this happens.

In Guatemala the corpses of street children have been found with their eyes burned out and ears and tongues cut out.

In countries as far apart as Peru and Sri Lanka schoolchildren have "disappeared" after being arrested by security forces.

In Liberia, many children have been arbitrarily killed or mutilated by the government and its opponents.

In South Africa, about 10,000 children were detained without charge or trial between 1985 and 1987.

All over the world, children are imprisoned, tortured and killed by the governments which should be guaranteeing their rights.

In the face of such horror, what can you do to help?

Firstly, become a member of Amnesty, it only costs £12. You can help directly by participating in our letter writing and urgent action campaigns.

We also need donations to enable us to continue our field investigations, to mount campaigns to free prisoners held illegally, to publicise abuses by governments and to give financial help to the families of victims.

Amnesty does get results.

Of the 29,000 prisoners-of-conscience whose cases we have taken up, 26,500 were successfully concluded.

In June, Brazil's President Collor de Mello said that his country should never again be cited by Amnesty International as his government would not tolerate human rights violations.

Sadly, our September newsletter contained many verbatim statements from Brazilian children who had been burned with cigarettes, tortured with scalding water and beaten.

We have to step up the pressure, not just on Brazil but all over the world, and to do this we must have your help.

The task is huge, our resources pitifully small.

Our whole year's advertising budget could not cover filming one 30 second TV commercial, let alone paying for it to be shown on commercial TV.

We can't afford many newspaper advertisements either.

Every pound we've scraped together to run this advertisement has to work hard to help little children who have nobody else to turn to. For their sakes, this advertisement must recruit 1,000 new Amnesty members and raise £100,000.

Please join us. Please be generous. Please give as much as you can. Please do it now.

I wish to be a member of Amnesty International. I enclose £12 Individual ☐
£15 Family ☐   £5 OAP ☐   £5 Student, Under 18, Claimant ☐
I wish to donate £100 ☐   £50 ☐   £25 ☐   £15 ☐   Other ☐

Mr/Ms._____

Address _____

_____ Postcode_____

To: Amnesty International British Section, FREEPOST, London EC1B 1HE.

AMNESTY INTERNATIONAL

Fig. 3a *An Amnesty International advertisement heading which forces you to read the text. Once read you cannot avoid filling in the coupon.*

(reversed out is white print on a black background). If you really must do this, make sure you see a proof. Is the meaning crystal clear?

The copy must make a connection between the headline (with supporting picture), and the coupon. It must answer the question, 'Why should I give you my money?' It is not an explanation of your organisation. Resist the temptation to say more than you need to. This is not a prestige advertisement. I doubt if you have show-rooms up and down the country where your supporters can express their concern, having remembered your advertisement. The main objective is direct response - it is not a funny joke or an attack on your competition. It describes what the problem is, how your organisation can solve it, and how the kind and gentle reader can help.

It is human and personal. Good copy is so well written you do not know you have just read it until you are writing out your cheque. It is a call to action for a very good reason. So, the writing flows. It is not stilted and does not talk up or down to its readership. It sounds like a friend. One of us!

The copy must be no longer than it needs to be to obtain a response. A single problem raised in the reader's mind will give an excuse for not giving. More than one and you are in trouble. Go through all copy looking for turn-off points. If in doubt, cut the word or phrase right out rather than trying to find an acceptable substitute.

When he or she is composing, your copywriter should think just like your supporters, and they should aim to use the same words and mental images that they do. It helps to brief the copywriter on the demographic profile of your supporters. The better the picture you can build up, the more effective the copy will be.

Use focus groups to discuss your advertising. This will enable you to cut across all those unpleasant truths that you have mentally screened out. Did no one respond because a plane crash was first in the news, or because your advertisement did not really make a convincing case for support? You know you have got it right when your existing supporters give to your advertisements. They are saying, 'This is why we joined! This is what we think is important!' Listen to them.

The picture

The picture, with the headline, should clearly convey as much as possible about the problem or the work concerned. Do make sure that you have the copyright for any picture you use. If you are using an agency picture which has featured in the media this can be expensive, but iconographic images that the reader has seen before will convey much more than a picture seen for the first time. Often disasters and problems are encapsulated in one image that comes to stand for the situation with all its complexities. For example, pictures of sick and malnourished prisoners behind barbed wire in Serbian camps once summed up the whole conflict in former Yugoslavia. Creating an image that does this for your cause will be a very powerful tool in persuading people to help you. You can let the picture state most of your argument, but it need not be shocking.

The ASA code of practice

If your cause is important, then something in your advertisement will probably shock, but it should not offend. Seek advice from the Advertising Standards Authority (ASA) if you are in any doubt. This will help to avoid the situation where you spend time and money creating an advertisement, only to find no one will use it because it contravenes the ASA code of practice. The code of practice is voluntary and, if you do offend, you will just be asked not to use that advertisement again; but being seen to infringe the code will not help to gain you support. Complaints are published, even if they are not upheld. Reply immediately to any enquiry from the ASA, as a delay in response can mean you are infringing the code. Bad publicity is much worse than good or even neutral publicity, and can damage your organisation.

You can obtain a copy of the code of practice from the ASA at Brook House, 2-16 Torrington Place, London WC1E 7HN.

The coupon

The coupon must be preceded by a call to action, such as 'Please join us today'. The customary 'today' is used to give urgency to the message. If the reader thinks they will send off the coupon next week it will languish, tucked into the side of the mantelpiece mirror, or simply never leave the newspaper. Direct mail letters have been used to carefully test different approaches and have shown that the simple psychology of giving a date by which the reply must be received ('Reply by the 27th and receive a free clock') or a reason for writing immediately ('Hurry whilst stocks last') increases the response very significantly. You can think of many ways of adding a note of urgency: 'Any delay means they will ...'

The coupon should make it abundantly clear just what you are asking for.

- If you would like a donation, say so, and suggest the amount. This is not the total amount of the appeal, which would just make an individual contribution look puny, but the amount you desire from each donor.

- It helps to give a variety of amounts with tick-boxes, which ensure commitment; and if, as often happens, there is no cheque enclosed, it enables you to write back effectively. The tick-boxes help people not to feel foolish about giving away a lot of money, and not to think you just need £5 (much of which will go in administering the donation).

- Have the highest amount on the left, so that people give the highest they feel comfortable with rather than the lowest. The theory is that, as people read from left to right, they will work their way along the line of boxes to the amount with which they feel comfortable. If the boxes are the other way around they will feel comfortable much earlier. Interestingly, however, most people seem to give the amount which is in the middle of the range. Circling the 'average' donation in the range can help to upgrade small donors.

- Make sure that the coupon is large enough for everyone to write their name and address clearly. Include 'postcode' in the address space because handwriting is often difficult to decipher, and the postcode is often the most legible part of the address. Use Mr, Ms or your preferred combination. This is very important, as later you could be laser printing these names, addresses and salutation on to an appeal letter. It is much more personal and effective if you can address people by their name rather than merely as 'Dear friend'.

- A FREEPOST address helps. Noone ever has a stamp to hand, and waiting to find or buy one means the urgency goes out of the appeal. If you wish to set up a FREEPOST address, contact your nearest Post Office manager. The address will be the same as your current address, apart from the postcode, and you can alter the rest as you like. The service is quite cheap. The words 'You do not have to use a stamp but it will save us postage' also seem to work for those who do have stamps to hand, and will save you money.

- Remember to put your name and logo on the

Fig. 3b *This shows that body copy is not everything. The headline and picture say it all.*

advertisement in large type. The vast majority of people who see your advertisement will not respond but, by associating your organisation with the copy, people will begin both to learn about your work and to think you are an active organisation. Your current members and donors will also gain that impression. In fact, members often return the coupon with a donation to show their support for the part of your work featured in the advertisement. Advertising looks like action.

It is essential to monitor the results of all your advertising. All your coupons should have a code on them signifying from which advertisement, in which newspaper, on which date, they have come.

Position on the page

The advertisement's position in the newspaper is important. Do not just buy the cheapest space. People read the papers selectively. If you are a third-world development organisation it makes sense to test the foreign news pages. Do not neglect the front page. It may be twice as expensive but nearly everyone reads it, and it has impact and memorability, yielding results that are often more than twice as good as those from other spaces.

Test space rigorously, but remember that this is difficult because the news has a habit of changing each day.

Research questionnaires

The simplest and most effective piece of pre-advertising research is to survey your existing membership. This can be done through a printed questionnaire placed in your newsletter with a letter of explanation and a FREEPOST envelope.

People love questionnaires, and you will continue to receive the replies for years after your closing date (heavily prompted with a note of urgency). You can ask a lot of questions. Thirty questions is not uncommon. Unless you can retain this information against your membership records (without offending the Data Protection Registrar) the survey should be completely anonymous. Expect at least one in five questionnaires back; sometimes as many as three in five are returned.

If you have the computer facilities to keep a mass of information on each member, then you can abandon anonymity and, using a window envelope, send the questionnaires out like direct mail with the name and address already on the form. This may reduce the rate of return, and will mean that your explanation of how you will use the data should be very clear and reasonable, but it will give you an excellent chance to segment and target those who respond. Some organisations waste no time and do this in their new members' pack.

In general your questions will ascertain the demographics of your donor-base. So you will find out:

- how old they are
- their gender
- what kind of education they have had

- what they do at work and play
- how much they earn
- which parts of your work they think are most important
- which newspapers and magazines they read. (A list for them to tick will indicate where you should advertise and place your loose-leaf inserts.)

Testing

Where to place your advertisement in the paper is not the only thing you should test. A key rule in fundraising, if not the key rule, is to test as much as possible. You don't really know anything until you have tested it. So, test concepts as well. Amnesty concentrates on individuals in its advertisements as a way of reaching the public; but it could concentrate on countries or themes like torture or political killing. There are probably many different ways of putting across your organisation's work.

With advertising, the difficulty of testing is that the response will vary depending on the paper you use, the position on the page and, most importantly, what else is featured in the press on that day. This means that exact testing is impossible. The willingness of people to support your organisation's work may not appear to be affected by what else is in the news, but be very careful. There could be several other charity advertisements in the same issue and one of them may relate to a news story, which may mean that readers are drawn to support someone else, or your cause appears insignificant by comparison.

Focus groups

Much use has been made of focus groups , and they are easy to arrange through an agency. The idea is that groups of your supporters and others, who have not joined, are brought together, usually in the evening with some food and drink, and asked their opinion of a variety of advertisements. This has to be done very skilfully. Unless you are an expert, the group will miraculously reflect your opinions straight back to you. In theory, focus groups should give you a real idea of why people are attracted to your adverts or put off by them. Your advertising agency should be able to arrange focus groups for you.

Sometimes, we have to take what people say with a bag of salt as they often act completely differently. Focus groups told Amnesty that their strong advertisements were a turn-off and that they would never read or respond to them. In practice, however, it is to the stronger advertisements that people have responded by actually joining.

This is not to say that you will learn nothing from focus groups. Amnesty learnt that people respond best if they can identify with just one individual (rather than read about dozens of people suffering), often saying that they felt they had to act to prevent another individual suffering in that way. If you can afford focus groups, try them out, and you will be surprised how informative they can be.

Direct mail

Direct mail is the archetypal gift from marketing to fundraising. It is a simple and easily understood way of raising funds and recruiting members. Its real beauty, however, lies in the ease with which you can test creative ideas in the real world with immediate feedback on how well they are doing. This very process has led, however, to a frightening similarity in most direct mail packages and it will tax all your innovative powers to devise new formats that work as well as the originals and make your appeal stand out.

Commonly referred to as junk mail, direct mail has a reputation for waste on a large scale. As direct mail agencies and list brokers (who will sell you lists of the names and addresses of thousands of potential prospects), as well as computers, become increasingly sophisticated this is becoming easier to avoid. My first experience of trying to introduce direct mail to an organisation was a curt reply from the director, 'Let me tell you we will never use direct mail here. Now, what else would you like to talk to me about?' It took quite a struggle to get direct mail back on that meeting's agenda, but the organisation went on to triple its membership, principally through the use of well targeted and executed direct mail packages.

The Post Office offers a good discount for bulk mailing, provided that you can put your letters in 'Mailsort order'. This should be discussed in detail with your PO representative, your mailing house and membership department. The only drawback is that you are required to print the ubiquitous Mailsort logo on your envelopes. Junk mail afficionados will treasure these letters, though a lot of other people never open them - but they probably would not respond to your appeal anyway. There are, however, lots of other postage stamps and logos to use, and for specialist mailings and especially short runs where you are expecting large donations it does help to make your whole package more attractive by having a real stamp or smart PO logo on the envelope.

Given the usual low costs of a direct mail pack and a reduced postage rate, it should be possible for you to at least break even if only 2% of those mailed respond. Remember, we are investing in new supporters, not making a profit from them. I have known many fundraisers despair because 95% of the people they mailed did not respond! To be a true fundraiser you must master the art of accepting rejection.

Keeping and using records

Keep as much information on your members as possible and write differently to as many of them as you can. It may not be very cost-effective to write separate letters to many different groups of members, but you can at least try by varying the tick boxes (which set out the amounts you are asking for) on your return coupon, according to the affluence of the people you are mailing or, better still, their past giving record. Why insult them by asking for £15 when they regularly give you £150? Why antagonise them by asking for £1,000 when they have only ever given you £15 at a time? If someone's regular donation is £50, starting the tick-boxes at £50 and working up will often give them the confidence to upgrade their gift.

The elements of the direct mail pack

The key elements of a direct mail pack are:

• a carefully designed outer envelope
• an appeal letter requesting help
• a reply coupon
• a FREEPOST envelope
• a leaflet telling the recipient more about the organisation.

The outer envelope

A good direct mail pack has an outer envelope with an intriguing phrase and picture, designed to appeal to those who may be interested in the organisation (and to let everyone else drop it in the bin).

A return address (which allows the Post Office to send back to you letters which are not deliverable) is very useful to you, as you can then update your list, taking off those who have 'gone away', etc. This includes the deceased, unknowns and Mr Angries.

The appeal letter

Typically these are four pages long, because tests have shown a four-page letter pulls better than fewer pages. In fact, the more pages the better; but remember that each paragraph must be compulsive reading, and that it is hard to write more than four pages keeping your readers with you. Most organisations find it impossible to achieve a satisfactory letter more than one page long - hence the surprising result that they have better returns from shorter ones. Shorter letters are at a disadvantage because after years of receiving four-page letters it appears to the reader that anything less isn't particularly important. If you ask people in focus groups which they prefer they will say short letters; but in practice they treat the longer letter as more important (provided every word is worthwhile and not just padding).

The format of the letter is simple. You present the problem directly, tell the reader exactly what is happening, so that they know just how appalling the problem is, then tell them how you are going to solve that problem and what they must do for you to succeed in this.

The opening paragraph and the PS are the most-read parts of a letter, so put your important messages there. The best advice I've received on writing is to:

• develop an idea of your target audience (your typical member or donor) and write for them - preferably for an individual reader whose needs you can identify.

Fig. 3c *Here Shelter uses a dramatic message which ensures you open the envelope willing to help.*

- keep your sentences reasonably short and the vocabulary accessible.
- use the active voice: 'The state prosecutor called for the death penalty', rather than 'The death penalty was called for by the state prosecutor' (Amnesty International style book). This is known to help readers and sustain their interest.
- avoid jargon unless you have to use it, and explain it when you must use it.
- allow access to the text by a clearly manifest structure. You will see this done in many direct mail letters by underlining and clear headings. Only underline what really needs emphasis.

Recently, there has been a back-to-basics move linked to the 'relationship' marketing concept. This emphasises writing real letters to people as if they were your friends - not heavily underlined, laser-printed letters with photos mixed in with the text. It seeks to create a relationship by making every contact as personal as possible, rather than considering your donors as a list of names and addresses with no independent needs or will.

The return coupon and FREEPOST envelope

The coupon should be a clear and simple device. A sheet of A5 paper (half A4 size) is usually enough. Do make sure that the return envelope is large enough for the coupon and a cheque to fit inside easily.

- Let the first words repeat the core message of the appeal letter: 'Yes, I would like to help ...' to confirm to the donor and the organisation what the appeal is for. This is now rather a hackneyed phrase and you should find one that is appropriate and true for your own work.

- Either be sure that the money will be used in exactly the way you say it will, or give yourself an opt-out, such as adding '... and for all our other important work'.

- The donor's address will already be on the coupon if you followed the ideas above. If not, lots of room should be left with a clear space for the postcode and Mr/Ms or whichever titles you use, so that you can personalise your letters later.

- The return FREEPOST address should be written out, just in case the FREEPOST envelope is lost or not inserted.

- The size of gift you are asking for should be made clear.

- If it is a prospecting appeal, all the ways for people to join or donate should be laid out, with simple tick-boxes to make the form easy and quick to fill in.

- If you accept credit cards let people know - and don't forget to count the boxes for the credit card number. Many designers get this detail wrong.

- Last, but not least, code every different mailing on the coupon so that you can analyse them.

The additional leaflet

One useful test you can conduct in prospecting packs, before rolling them out in tens of thousands, is whether it is worthwhile including an extra leaflet or other form of insert. It may well be that your letter is adequate and the extra cost of the leaflet is not worthwhile. Yet it may be that you cannot really say all you need to in the letter (even if it is four pages long!) and need more room without overburdening the letter. Perhaps, more importantly, you may need to add some pictures to show the situation clearly - both the problem and your solution to it. If enclosing a standard appeal leaflet, do not forget to remove the usual reply coupon, or you will confuse the prospect and your coding system will not work properly.

If you wish to show horrifying pictures of your work, you may consider putting them in a separate envelope inside the appeal, marked 'This envelope contains distressing pictures which may shock you'. I am told that the device has worked very well for the NSPCA, among others.

A campaigning action, as mentioned above, could also be used. Try testing the insertion of a postcard to send, calling for action to help relieve the problem you are engaged on.

Addressing direct mail

Last, but a long way from least, is the address. The most common way to handle this is to produce Cheshire labels (a common brand of label which is easy for mailing house machinery to handle) for your mailing house, which they will fix onto your return coupon in such a position that the labels show through the window envelopes. (You can also laser print the address onto the coupon, and also, possibly, the letter. This allows you to personalise the appeal; but it is expensive to add the address to the coupon as well - hence the multitude of appeal letters with the coupon attached to the foot of the letter.)

Printing the address on the coupon and using a window envelope, then, avoids printing the address twice. You need the address on the reply coupon to build up your records for segmentation and measuring the success of each mailing. People will rarely bother to write it on the coupon themselves, and if they try to it will slow them down and confuse your membership department because people write their addresses differently each and every time. Printing the address also allows people to let you know if you have their name and address recorded incorrectly.

'Gone away.'

Some organisations remail all the 'gone away' addresses on the grounds that people of a similar nature will have moved into the house. Personally, I'm not convinced by this. If it were true we could mail all the streets where our supporters have lived and double our membership overnight. People have very different psychologies despite living in similar houses. However, as I have never tested the concept I really cannot truly claim to know whether it works or not.

If you have bought a list and more than 3% turn out to be 'gone aways' you should be able to obtain some compensation from the agency that sold you the list. If it is your own list you must ensure that you are paying attention to all the letters that you receive from your supporters. It is very expensive for you, and irritating for your supporters, if you mail 'gone aways' repeatedly. If you are receiving letters that say, 'I've told you three times my husband is deceased,' you have a serious problem in your membership department that requires immediate attention.

Mailing from abroad

There are many fine books on direct mail, so I will not go into exhaustive detail here, but among the ideas you could try is reducing the postage by mailing from an appropriate country abroad. The foreign stamp may help to get your envelope opened. The problems with this are that under the international postal rules you cannot use a UK return address and so the Post Office will not return the 'gone aways'; the cost of shipping your printing abroad could be high; and printing in a foreign country for the first time may not be a rewarding experience. The lower cost of postage from abroad can, however, save you a lot of money, and help turn your appeal into a success by increasing the response rate even a trifle. (Postage from the USA, for example, can be much cheaper than posting within the UK!)

Varying your appeals

Vary your appeals, so that your members do not get bored with them but believe that you are sending them out because you have a real need, not just because it's time for another appeal. At the same time you must keep the format fairly close to a personal letter. (Though beware of becoming too friendly and losing the strength of an appeal.)

Advocacy

Advocacy within appeals in not necessarily a bad thing, though if you give someone a list of ways to help, they will probably choose the easiest. Returning a pre-printed postcard is much easier than locating a cheque book. Inviting an action may, however, encourage people to give who have never given before, as the action may draw them into reading the appeal. Test it for yourself. (I regret to say I have even lost money on an appeal because it looked too much like a campaigning appeal, asking people to write letters instead of sending in money. Spurred on by some success in adding advocacy to appeal letters I had helped create a pack which suggested several useful actions that could be taken, lost amongst which was the appeal for cash.)

One idea is to link an action with a donation. Amnesty has tried split cards which the donor tears in two, sending one half to Amnesty to give or join. This half says, 'I have today sent a letter to such and such a government.' The other half, saying, 'I have today joined, or donated, to Amnesty International', is sent to the government concerned, which lets them know the person's depth of feeling. (See also Chapter 4 —'How effective is advocacy?')

Style

Once you have an established style to your appeals, think about the variations that will make each appeal different.

- Pick a different theme for each appeal - for example, starvation, torture, rain forest destruction; or use geography: Africa, India, Brazil, London.
- Instead of illustrating the problem by reference to individuals, refer to communities; though be careful with this, because focus group tests report that people are very often drawn to support charities through identification with individuals. This is often summed up by fundraisers as 'people give to people not organisations'.
- Vary the person doing the asking, from your director or chairperson to an appropriate celebrity or relevant statesperson. This is sometimes done by adding an additional 'lift' letter from that person, which gives a personal

message to strengthen the appeal. Such celebrity endorsement has become so common that it is really only useful if the celebrity really has an appropriate connection and is well known enough to your members to make a difference.

- Vary the size of envelope, as well as the enclosures.
- Vary the linking element (which unites all the enclosures and the envelope together). Often this is just a common phrase or campaign logo, but it does help to show you are not just putting the same old appeal out again.

Linking appeals

Linking appeals with each other is useful: 'We asked you for money for a new school bus in June. Now winter has set in, and it has broken down. The children are trudging through the snow.'

Making sure that your communications are clearly from one and the same organisation will significantly increase your income in the long term.

Write up the results of each appeal in your newsletter and thank your donors. Show how the money was spent and the successes that ensued. Do not be afraid to ask people, 'Look out for the next appeal because its very important'. All too often newsletters and appeals appear to come from different organisations.

Incentivisation

Incentivising appeals works the same as other fundraising incentive schemes. The incentive should be appropriate to the organisation (and, if possible, the appeal itself), and used to indicate a higher than usual level of contribution. Its effectiveness will wear off if used constantly.

The World Wide Fund for Nature (WWF) has traditionally sent out car-stickers in all its appeals, and these can be seen advertising the organisation in every traffic jam and car park. Unlike incentives offered in return for a gift, these are freely sent out on the inertia basis, ie. having received a gift the recipient will feel like responding generously in return. They also give free publicity, but only because the scale of WWF mailings is so huge that they will appear over and over again.

Loose-leaf inserts

Loose-leaf inserts are leaflets inserted in the pages of magazines or newspapers. They are not bound in, and often fall out when the periodical is first opened. Some people hold their magazines open over the wastepaper bin to facilitate this process.

Loose-leaf inserts can become a mainstay of your recruitment campaigns. You will find that they have a relatively low response rate, but because they are inexpensive a rate of only 0.25% should be sufficient to break even. A single sheet of A4 paper, folded twice, is customary, though many other variations are tried. Some even come complete with gummed edges so that the return coupon can be sent back without need of an envelope. You will find this more expensive, but it is easier for the potential member or donor to send it back to you and those few extra returns can be crucial.

As in advertising, a striking picture on the front cover helps to capture attention, and a good headline will lead people to read the rest of your text. This must be simple and easy to read, leading straight to the coupon. Like an advertisement, a loose-leaf insert should have a FREEPOST address, making it easy to return.

A topical insert seems to work excellently close to the event but, as magazines have long lead times, you will find this is difficult to arrange. Amnesty has tried the deep emotional pull that works in its national newspaper advertising, but that still cannot out-pull the 'banker leaflet ', (which simply represents the core work of the organisation), except in a very few publications. Interestingly, these are the ones with a simple phrase on the cover and no picture. They just ask the question, 'What is the best way to help a victim of brutal injustice?'

The ingredients of a good leaflet

The copy needs to move from a clear statement of the problem, to a description of what the organisation will do to solve the problem to how the donor can contribute. Pictures always help. You can use a lift-letter written into a leaflet in the same way as you do in a direct mail appeal but you do have much less space to make your case so it should be succinct and convincing.

If you are not using a professional copywriter, carefully read as many inserts as you can manage (I would suggest at least two dozen) and note down the most telling points that really affect you - but do not assume they have all worked well! Think about the 'angle' used to put the points across. Is it an anonymous voice, an authoritative voice, the director, a victim? What do the pictures show - success, the problem, happy faces, suffering people? You should ask yourself, how does the copy lead the reader to respond?

Testing

Apart from being cheap, the best thing about inserts is that they are easily tested. You can insert three different kinds into the same magazine (each with a different code on the coupon, of course) and judge which works best. But often, a magazine will only sell you the whole run and not allow you to insert just a few thousand at a time. Amnesty have run over two million inserts in various magazines for a few years now, and still test out new ideas and concepts to keep a fresh look in front of the public.

If you do not already know what works best for you (and to really know you must have proved it by proper testing of alternatives), then you must test each concept for yourself. Be careful: in a two-way split test you can only test one

Fig. 3d *Three leaflets testing different approaches. An emotional appeal about children, a topical appeal about Tiannamen Square and a generic appeal about Prisoners of Conscience. In which media do you think these would work best?*

idea against one other, and if there is more than one difference you will not know which was responsible for the improvement. You can test three ideas or more against each other, providing they are in the same medium at the same time, as long as they are on different inserts and are separately coded.

Special points

The mechanical process that lifts and inserts the leaflets often needs an edge to grip and paper of a certain size. Do check with the magazine that they can accept your leaflet, making sure they have seen a sample, before you commit yourself to a large print bill. This is a must if there is anything at all unusual about the size or shape of your insert.

You never have a nil response. So, if nothing comes back, the inserts have either not reached the magazine or have not been inserted. It is best to make sure your agency or mailing house is committed to seeing that everything arrives at the magazines before their deadlines. If you have many tests going on in several magazines it can be a nightmare for a busy fundraiser to check everything is where it should be, when it should be.

If you are inserting in the weekend supplements or a newspaper you will see a distressing quantity of your precious leaflets strewn down the street. Be prepared for this as people are very careless of their environment. It may make you think twice about such inserts; but do wait until you see the actual results before making a decision.

Member-gets-member schemes

An easy and most obvious way to recruit lots of new members is by asking your existing supporters to sign up all their friends and colleagues. This is probably already happening if you did but know it. The people most likely to join are those just like your present supporters, and people tend to make friends with people just like themselves.

There are all sorts of ways of spurring on this process. You can simply ask your members to sign up their friends but it helps, as usual, to make it easy for them. One way of doing this is to mail them several letters that they can send on to their friends with a suggestion that they join. This is best done in a separate direct mail package with a covering letter explaining just how important it is to your organisation to recruit new members, and that the most likely new members are those known to your existing supporters.

Make sure that your copy flows naturally through the exercise. It is easy to assume that you can simply ask for something like this to be done without talking about the serious problems you are trying to solve, and how this will help. It will be quite an effort for people, and they need to be convinced it is really important and will lead to an improvement in the situation with which you are dealing.

If you make the letters you enclose self-sealing so that they just need addressing, it will increase the number sent, but can cost a lot more. The cutting and gluing process is not cheap. Shop around for the most cost-effective supplier, but do check the proofs carefully, because the quality can vary enormously. If you are using colour, you should always ask to see a colour proof.

This is a fundraising exercise that really benefits from a creative approach. But be careful not to get carried away with ingenious ideas. I have tried sending beautiful colour postcards to supporters for them to send on, but it did not work very well, and I suspect the postcards were so good they went straight up on people's walls - though it may have failed because the cards did not allow enough space for people to send a personal message to their friends. I have tried asking people to copy their friends' names and addresses at Christmas time when they had their filofaxes open to write their cards; and I have also approached new members to send in a short list of their friends who might join. These approaches work, provided you take care that the materials are good and the exercise looks as if it's really important, not just in-house photocopying and a plain letter. But none of them have ever worked as well as when people approach their friends directly.

The best method of all is to have your supporters approach their friends face-to-face. This is the most effective way of raising funds in any case, even if only a few members take part.

If you have an appeal for donations going out to your supporters every month, it may be more effective to insert your member-gets-member scheme in your newsletter. Then it will not clash with an appeal, and has the bonus of saving a considerable amount on postage; but do bear in mind the general rule that it will be much more effective if mailed on its own. As a direct mail appeal to your members will bring in much more profit in the short term, you should not substitute a member-gets-member scheme for an appeal.

Once again, keep testing ideas and checking what other organisations are doing.

Member and donor recruitment: general issues

I have chosen to look at member and donor recruitment together because the techniques are so similar. You may have the luxury of giving your supporters the choice of joining or just donating, but if you choose the latter course you will still need to keep your donors informed and pleased about their relationship with you, if you are to maximise your income. A donors' newsletter is just as important as the members' newsletter. Because the members' newsletter is often long established and run by another department with its own objectives, it is often more cost-effective to recruit donors and reach them through a new newsletter that you design and control yourself.

The key difference between members and donors is the political difference that members usually have voting rights and donors do not. Members are also inclined to think of themselves as long-term participants in the organisation, and the organisation will often think of them in terms of work that they can do rather than the income they will generate.

Those organisations such as political parties and pressure groups that look to their members to carry out campaigning work (commonly called 'advocacy') will often set up local groups, and it is in those local groups that the real work is done by dedicated individuals who have the time and inclination for such activity. On the part of these activists there is often a degree of resentment, of which you should be keenly aware, when they are asked for additional funds. They frequently see themselves as giving their time rather than their money. This attitude is often also found among staff, who are fearful of upsetting members by the use of fundraising techniques which they see as a bad thing per se or a necessary evil at best. Some relief can be obtained from this if you are able to separate out the activists from the national members (some of whom will, of course, be or become activists), and if you can allow people to opt out of your appeals to members. Flag the activist carefully on your database and consider carefully when, and how, to approach them for funds.

If your targeting of prospects is accurate you will no doubt mail a few of your existing members, asking them to join. This is sometimes taken personally, but even with the best de-duplicating system currently available it is unavoidable to some degree.

Another occurrence in prospecting is that you may find that certain lists or publications are more likely to provide members and others more likely to provide donors. If you only require one or the other, test the media carefully and adapt your literature to suit your requirements. Think about adapting your organisation to their needs.

Reminders to lapsed members

All your recruitment will be in vain if you fail to retain your members. An efficient subscription reminder system is essential. One or two reminders sent out occasionally will not do. Many of your members will simply not notice them. In survey after survey many lapsed members have said, 'I thought I was a member,' or, 'You have not sent me a reminder.' This is partly because they belong to many organisations and cannot remember which they have a standing order with and which they sent a cheque to last week. It is also because the best organisations send out five reminders, and, as people become accustomed to that, anything less is not taken seriously. Of course, it may also be that your administration is at fault.

Join several organisations like your own, let your membership lapse and see what happens. Note when you stop receiving their newsletter and when you stop receiving their appeals. (Lapsed members are a very important source of donations - but only those who have a consistent record of giving in the past. Find out which from your database!) Keep all their reminder letters and compare their programme with your own. There is always something to learn.

A good 'reminders' procedure is to send:

1 an 'early bird' reminder a month before the renewal is due. This can increase your revenue by bringing forward some subscriptions by a month (much to the confusion of your administration), but more importantly, it will stop their renewal drifting by a month

2 a second reminder ('Renew now!') at the time of lapsing

3 a final reminder one month later.

The last two reminders are sent to those segments of the donor-base that are worth renewing. Each stage should be costed against the income from members rejoining, over their expected new lifetime with the organisation. Those people who give very generously are worth sending many more reminders to than those who never give at all.

You should also test additional reminders to see if they are cost-effective. This must take into account the lifetime value of those renewing and not just the immediate income. (Lifetime value of a supporter is their average donation per year multiplied by their average lifetime with you.)

Lapsed donors

Many organisations have adopted the same procedure with donors as with members. Renewing their donations is a little different, but the difference is only in the copy. Reminding them that a year ago they gave a donation, and inviting them to do the same thing again, can be much appreciated. The number of reminders needs careful testing, and it may be much better to move on quite quickly to appeals for specific work rather than issuing generic reminders about a donation.

Telemarketing to lapsed supporters

Telemarketing is a great way to bring back countless members. I have listened in to many calls in which the lapsed member is charmed to receive an avuncular call, from the organisation they supported, enquiring why they have left and asking them to kindly rejoin.

It is possible to bring people back at a much higher rate of subscription than they lapsed at, to be paid usually by direct debit or standing order. Prospects should be asked first for, say, £10 per month, to give the richer members the opportunity of giving at that level; then £5 per month, and lastly for the fee they lapsed at. At the moment £5 per month is a common average, which improves on the usual donation or annual fee of £15 to £20.

For your key donors (or donating members) it may be well worth phoning them soon after they have lapsed, to enquire why. They will appreciate the effort you have taken. Lapsing may be due to changed financial circumstances, in which case they are then likely to rejoin when their circumstances improve; or it may be that they have just retired, in which case you may well learn about a legacy. You may also be able to sort out a problem or misunderstanding that they have with your organisation.

It is not unusual to have some 80% of people pledging to rejoin, but sometimes only half of those will eventually come through. It is worth flagging on your database those members brought back by telemarketing, as they will be susceptible to telemarketing appeals in the future.

There are now several companies that specialise in telemarketing for charitable organisations. It is well worth using these, unless you have real expertise, because this is such a powerful approach that it will upset your supporters if not done with sensitivity. You will always experience a number of complaints, as with any fundraising technique. Any call, however mild and apologetic, will make a few people complain. This is most likely to happen at the beginning of a campaign when the callers are getting used to their scripts and are a little wooden.

Resting actors are a good choice as callers, as they are used to working from a script and have pleasant voices. Do work carefully on the script with your agency, and test it before rolling it out on all your lapsed members.

Telemarketing for philanthropic organisations has blossomed since 1990, but we are still far from realising its full potential. Most organisations still think of it only as part of their renewal programme because that affects lapsed members, on the basis that if these people are offended it doesn't really matter. This is a self-defeating philosophy because it locks out a wide range of telemarketing activity. Almost anything you do by letter can be done by phone - more quickly and with a better response rate.

Naturally, this costs more and you need to test its cost-effectiveness. Organisations that use telemarketing a lot often use it to precede an appeal, letting people know how important the appeal is. Alternatively, you can send a letter saying that a call is on its way. This may spur the recipient to action and avoid the expense of the call.

The future of telemarketing

As thousands of people renew their subscriptions to dozens of organisations after telemarketing, we are becoming a telephone responsive society. This is also becoming manifest in the number of credit card purchases made over the phone, from buying theatre tickets to sending flowers by Interflora. In Chapter 10 we will look at future stages of this development, including interactive TV and the communications superhighway.

§

Recruiting new supporters can be a humbling experience. Most people will say no. Often 99 % of people will automatically say no or even 99.9 % but that 1% or even 0.1% can be enough to build a mighty organisation solving immense human or environmental problems. If you know how much an individual's lifetime support is worth you can often face such external rejection with equanimity. Knowing their worth and the effort taken to recruit them, you will also be able to recognise just how vital it is to retain them, to fulfil the trust you have engendered and that they have placed in your organisation.

4 Inside the Pyramid: Developing your Supporters

Appeals to your supporters

The best known method of obtaining additional funds from your members or donors is to write to them. As a substantial proportion will have been recruited this way, and an even larger proportion will have joined or donated to another organisation this way, you have a very warm prospect list sensitised to direct mail and therefore likely to respond to this method.

Appeals to members are very similar to prospecting letters. Naturally, you are dealing with a sympathetic and knowledgeable audience, although, if your organisation is rapidly expanding, it is unwise to expect too much sophisticated knowledge from the new members, who will also be the most likely to give. You should be careful to explain all those internal references and inscrutable acronyms.

This means that you should appeal not just for the organisation in general, but for new, real needs that they would not expect their membership fee or initial donation to cover. This is possibly the most important factor in appeals. They must come across as genuine pleas for additional urgently needed funds, not just the usual bi-monthly appeal for more money.

Successful organisations typically appeal between four and six times in the year, often sending a newsletter between the appeals. The number of appeals can be increased until the return begins to drop below the cost. In some organisations it is quite possible to appeal twelve times in the year. Most members are likely to be paid monthly, and a combination of direct mail appeals with a monthly giving programme and 'soft' fundraising in the newsletter will provide a greater variety of interest for the members. Soft fundraising includes raffles, legacy appeals, merchandising catalogues and member-gets-member schemes.

The covering envelope

As with all direct mail work, some thought needs to go into this.

- A return address is important (it need not go on the front of the envelope); and make sure your membership department is ready to adjust the changes in names and addresses from returned envelopes, which are usually marked 'gone away'.

- A window envelope is useful, as you can then place the name and address on the return coupon (positioned to show through the window) and save people the chore of writing it out for you - which they will inevitably do in a way that differs slightly from your records. The resulting confusion can last for years. Sometimes the donor will just return a cheque without filling in their name, and if you have no name and address your records will not be able to allocate the gift correctly. This will also cost you dearly if you begin donor clubs based on amounts previously given, and you need to issue end-of-year letters thanking people for their help. (In the US that letter forms the basis for the charitable tax returns which are deductible against American income tax. Americans giving to a UK charity will also appreciate this consideration from you).

- Imaginative envelope design can be very effective. An appropriate picture and phrase helps recipients realise what the contents are about and should entice them to open the envelope, but be careful not to mislead them into thinking the appeal is something else entirely. They will not be well disposed towards you if they feel they have been deceived into opening the letter. Different sizes, colours and textures of envelopes are useful in making a distinction between different approaches, and avoid your appeals seeming like a routine affair.

Naturally, you should use the Post Office's Mailsort system to keep your costs down, unless you are mailing to a special group who you feel should receive something special. (Short runs are not liable for the Mailsort discount). Then a real postage stamp or one of the Post Office's special stamps will be appropriate and make the recipient feel more personally approached. A first-day cover can be used to great effect if it is relevant to the organisation. Contact the Post Office to discuss the possibility of a special stamp - though they do have a long waiting list, and very few organisations are likely to be accepted. You can also have your logo on the Post Office cancellation stamp - at a cost.

The letter

Ideally you should select the most highly respected person in your organisation to sign the letter - but not to write it, which should always be done by a copywriter. It will not work unless it is written specifically to bring in donations, and the sincerity and enthusiasm for the work to be done with that money must be clearly apparent. These are definitely not thank-you letters or progress reports, which should be kept separate from appeals.

Fig. 4a *Moving text, strong images, theme graphics and a clear ask. This pack has it all!*

The basic format of the letter is a statement of

- the need
- what your organisation can do about it
- how the donation will be used
- a very clear request for money.

Supporting material

Lots of other things can be added, but they should all build up the case for the donation and be specially designed, not just added because they are around at the time.

THE OBSERVER

CHELSEA BRIDGE HOUSE QUEENSTOWN ROAD

Dear Amnesty Supporter,

People ask me if I get personally involved with the news I cover.

Well, every good journalist tries to be impartial and not to take sides on an issue. But it's impossible to remain aloof from some of the tragedies in the world today.

Like you, I hoped the changes in the former Eastern Bloc would mean new freedoms and reduce Amnesty's work. But the conflicts in Yugoslavia show that just the opposite has happened. And the problems haven't faded in other parts of the world. Human rights continue to be abused in Iraq, in Somalia, and in too many other countries.

Today Amnesty is needed more than ever. Like every journalist involved in current affairs, I pay attention when an envelope bearing the Amnesty logo lands on my desk. I know an Amnesty press release will contain a vital news story- one that touches people's hearts. And most important, I know it will be reliable and accurate.

Amnesty know that publicity is vital in bringing cases of injustice before the world. And they are brilliant at it.

**The miracle is that Amnesty achieves
all this with such limited resources**

News organisations spend fortunes on trivial stories that are forgotten in 24 hours. Yet Amnesty must watch every penny in checking the facts about cases that are of real importance and urgency. At the same time it must investigate cases in far-off places sometimes at great personal risk.

There is no doubt that Amnesty's efforts achieve great good. When Amnesty speaks the world listens. I shudder to think of the consequences for freedom if Amnesty's voice is ever silenced for lack of finance. And right now, when Amnesty is needed so much, its own funding is under threat. With the world recession many international supporters aren't able to send donations as often as they would like.

Let me thank you for your continued support of Amnesty. And please, please be generous when you complete your donation form today.

Adrian Hamilton
Deputy Editor

Fig. 4b *An occasional lift letter from a celebrity or authority adds interest and integrity to your appeals.*

A lift letter from an appropriate celebrity can help a great deal, as can a leaflet showing the problem in pictures. Imaginative and money spinning additions have included a piece of opaque plastic to demonstrate the effect of cataracts; postcards to MPs protesting at the problem and saying, ' I have today given a donation to help'; and harrowing pictures sent in a separate envelope clearly marked 'Harrowing pictures: do not open if you may be upset'. Personally, I have always been drawn to maps, and find them a very useful and effective addition to an appeal that has a world-wide basis.

As usual, always test such material by sending out a separately coded control pack, without the enclosure, and seeing which is more productive. Then you will really learn about your donors' preferences and increase your effectiveness and fundraising skills. Try testing something in each appeal.

The FREEPOST envelope

Make it easy for your donors and give them a FREEPOST envelope in which to return their cheque. They will also use it to return letters of complaint, and sometimes stuff the whole appeal back into the envelope before returning it to you, in the mistaken belief that this is an environmentally sensitive gesture, but those envelopes will also turn up months and even years later with generous donations.

Try to make the return envelope part of the whole pack by designing it anew each time. Occasionally I have seen appeal papers which are cleverly converted into envelopes for re-use in returning a donation. This is fine as a one-off but is unlikely to be effective each time, as the appeals will begin to lack variety.

The return coupon

Arguably, this is the most important part of the appeal, and deserves quite as careful copywriting and design as any other part of it.

• Give the donor a voice by saying something the donor can identify with. Commonly this is on the lines of, 'Yes, I enclose a donation to support your work for ...' , but I am sure that you can easily improve on that.

• Emphasise the amount you are requesting. This is usually done with a short line of tick boxes to help the donor feel that they are doing the right thing, rather than being mean by giving too little or foolish by giving too much.

• Help your donors by setting out all the possible ways to pay, including credit card donations and any credit card hotline that you can set up.

• Most importantly, enter the member's name and address on the coupon, using laser, Cheshire labels, or whatever process looks good and is accurate and cost-effective.

• Remember to code each coupon so that you will know from which appeal it has been returned, and which segment of your donor-base it has come from. If you are sophisticated enough to segment your appeals into different categories, try mailing each segment with an appeal for donations the size of which is based on the donors', or groups of donors', past giving record.

Time of year

Whether the time of year makes a difference or not is highly debatable. For example, most fundraisers will avoid August, as a large percentage of your target audience will be away enjoying their holidays - yet many fundraisers will claim to have had their best appeal in August.

Perhaps this was due to the quality of that appeal, or perhaps there was no competition. Will people arriving home from their holiday feel rested and in a generous mood, or will they be fed-up with the prospect of returning to work, and broke?

Many organisations appeal before Christmas and this makes sense, as it is traditionally a time of goodwill and giving to charity. Your supporters are more likely to give to you than someone else, but they won't if you don't ask them.

Again, many fundraisers claim to do well in January, because there is no competition and people are relaxed, perhaps feeling guilty after the Christmas indulgences, and, on opening a fresh wage packet, inclined to be generous. On the other hand, many fundraisers think that this is too soon after the Christmas appeals and people need January to get over the usual Christmas extravagances.

Thank-you letters

This is a most important part of the appeal because it is the first step to the next donation and, as usual, it should be appropriate and prompt. If you can tell your supporters how well the appeal is going and how much you have accomplished so far, you may receive further donations.

The thank-you letter shows that you care about the individuals gift, so make sure it is not merely a poor photocopy that devalues the gift. A real letter, signed by the person who signed the appeal letter and referring to the basis of the appeal, is important and will help to build a lasting relationship. It does help if you can quote the exact amount received. Be sure that your software has this capability.

Monthly giving

Monthly giving is a crucial step in ensuring the long-term financial stability of your NGO. It works on the simple proposition that, because most people are paid monthly, it is easier for them to give, say, £10 per month than £50 out of one month's salary. Of course this means that twelve months later you have received £120 instead of £50. More importantly, because monthly giving is either by standing order or by direct debit, you will receive £120 the next year, and the next, and the next, until the order is cancelled. Naturally, there is an attrition rate as people face financial problems, but that is surprisingly low compared to annual giving.

If your organisation is a charity and the monthly gift is by means of a covenant, then this will last for a minimum of four years and your organisation can reclaim the tax. This is a slightly complicated procedure that seems to baffle many finance departments, who pile up unclaimed tax year after year. Each donor does have to be asked to fill out a short form each year. The Charities Aid Foundation (CAF) will undertake this work for you for a fee, but this is much better than not claiming the tax at all, which happens surprisingly often.

Technically, covenants can be 'variable' by being linked to another event, e.g., the royalties from a book or interest rates. It is not a good idea to encourage these complicated schemes unless large sums are involved and there is a real reason for such linkage which meets the needs of your donor rather than being a fanciful whim.

At least one major NGO owes its financial survival to the power of monthly giving, which persisted at a serious level long after the cynic would have thought all links with the organisation would be cut.

If you do not run six appeals in the year, then slotting in a monthly giving programme is easy. If you have reason to believe that your supporters will not accept another appeal, you are faced with the possibility of either replacing an appeal (in which case monthly giving will probably bring in less in the first year,

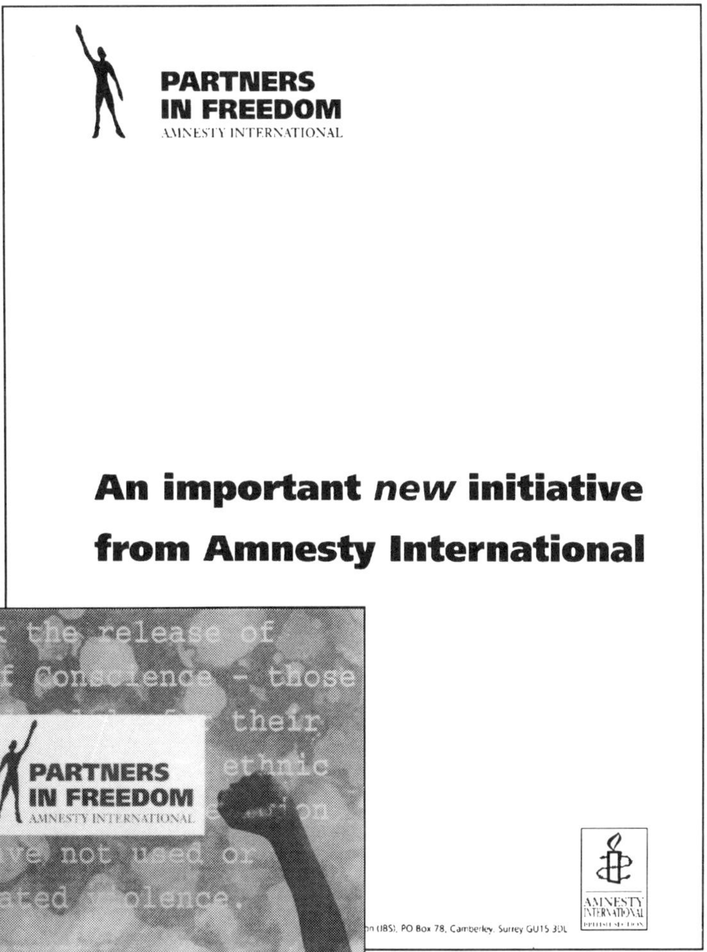

An important *new* initiative
from Amnesty International

Fig. 4c *A pre-appeal phone call to high donors or a postcard can dramatically improve response. Test it.*

Fig. 4d *"Partners in Freedom" are the armchair activists who could play a key role in financing your organisation. Research their needs well - and don't neglect to fulfill them!*

but will more than justify itself thereafter), or taking the higher givers out of your appeal programme and sending them the monthly giving shot.

A hotly debated question is whether monthly givers should be sent appeals as well. Some organisations make a selling point of not sending appeals, but I have noticed that monthly givers soon miss their thank-you letters and the feeling of involvement that comes from responding to an appeal, and begin donating again. They also forget just which organisation they have a monthly arrangement with, which organisation they pay their fees to by direct debit - and often forget completely whether or not they have renewed their subscription.

Forms of monthly giving

The basic form of monthly giving is a donor club whose members give a certain amount per month and receive special thanks in the form of privileges. These can be as small as a smart lapel badge, or as much as you can afford to give back without nullifying the gift. If the organisation is a zoo, for example, privileges can extend to spending time with certain animals outside of normal visiting hours, feeding and grooming them along with the keepers, meeting the head keeper and discussing future developments, etc.

Different monthly rates

At this point monthly giving and 'big gift' giving programmes are very similar. You will need to make a clear distinction so that your supporters are not confused. Usually the difference resides in the numbers giving and the level of donation. Monthly giving lies at the mass end of that spectrum.

You should aim to bring as many people as possible into the monthly giving programme, and you can run schemes with different rates and different rewards. Most of the basic schemes are at the £5 or £10 a month level, though much has also been done recently in asking people to give around £50 a month. That is, obviously, a much greater commitment and you will need to have a very significant reason for asking for that amount, and a very special programme for those givers to enjoy. At that level they will probably need to feel a very important part of the organisation, as indeed they will be. You will also need to ensure that your service to those people is faultless and of a high quality that lasts for all the years you would like to keep on receiving those funds.

Ideally, the higher givers will be treated as a separate part of the donor-base and all communications to them will recognise that they are members of that special group. You may need to set up a separate mailing system and write a special newsletter for them as well. All this will be well worthwhile but, naturally, you should test the appeal on a small segment of the base first to get the proposition right. In particular, you will want to know how much to ask for and what to offer in return. As this is difficult to do in practice, a focus group could be used. The Greenpeace 'Frontline' programme is of this nature, appealing to the armchair activist with videos and special reports that put them in the front line.

Big gifts

The process of treating the higher givers as a separate 'club' bridges the gap between monthly giving and big gifts proper, because membership of these clubs can be through a substantial fee or its equivalent monthly donation. The importance of upgrading your donors into these clubs, or attracting potential major donors into them, cannot be overstressed. These high level clubs are the recruiting ground for your major gift programme: they can yield not only substantial annual income, but also funds for major capital appeals.

Approaching major donors

Once potential major donors are identified from among the prominent members of high value clubs, or by such techniques as matching your supporters' names against lists of wealthy individuals, or systematically following up the networks of contacts that your influential supporters all have, you must make sure that they identify closely with your organisation's goals before you approach them.

Prospects can be invited to open days, prestigious events, dinners and any other occasion at which you have the opportunity to explain to them your vision of the future of your organisation, and to enhance their understanding of your work. To maximise your chances of success, you need to know your prospect's current appreciation of your work, and to be able to convince them of the necessity of the next steps you propose. When you feel that you both share the same goals for the work of the organisation, then you are in a position to set up the 'ask' for the maximum amount that the individual will be happy to give. All this requires knowing your prospects in depth, and in particular knowing how to meet their needs for knowledge and recognition.

The ask is best made face-to-face by a friend or colleague of the prospect who is in the same peer group or profession and who has already given themselves. It can be done in the prospect's office, or wherever they feel comfortable. It is important to have a set sum in mind, or at least a range of giving options, but do not forget that gifts in kind, and secondments of staff or use of building space can be invaluable too.

In some charities such work is undertaken by Board members, who have been offered a place on the Board for this specific purpose and who have the task of big gift fundraising written into their job descriptions. Do ensure that the people you engage to make the ask really can ask for money from the right prospects. It is wise to run a short training programme for them, in which they brush up their knowledge of the organisation, its successes and its future needs, and their knowledge of the prospects. In the course of the programme they should have the chance to practice asking for money. This will be unnecessary for some, who will be adept at calling in favours and who enjoy the game, but it will be vital for those who are less sure or practised at fundraising.

Capital appeals

The ultimate programme is a capital appeal, which I will not dwell on in detail here, as Marion Allford's excellent book *Charity Appeals* will tell you all you need to know.

If, however, you are thinking of raising a large amount of money for something like the purchase of a new building, then it is a good idea to undertake a feasibility study first. This will help to prevent the waste of time and effort as well as any serious disturbance to your key supporters that may result from a premature appeal. The time spent will not be wasted if it is shown that an appeal is likely to succeed, as the consultants' interviews with key supporters will help to advance the appeal. It is well worthwhile seeking out a reputable firm of consultants who have undertaken several such appeals for organisations similar to yours. The Institute of Charity Fundraising Managers (ICFM) has a list of charity consultants which they will supply on request.

Big gift committees

One simple system is to group your key donors in a committee. The chairman must give financially, and so must each committee member, or they will not be effective in asking others to give. They should meet three times only in the following six to nine months to:

1 list at least six people they are going to ask for substantial funds; and decide how much they expect to receive. (This avoids the same people being approached twice.)

2 list persons whom they have approached, any additional prospects they can propose, and any people not yet approached.

3 tidy up those final requests and thank all the committee members for their generous support in raising such a huge amount.

Keys to success

The key to the whole thing is a persuasive chairperson, who has the clout and integrity to both ask the right people onto the committee and ensure they undertake their tasks. In particular, the follow-up work the chairperson does a couple of weeks before the second meeting is crucial. Here he may need to call on the services of the staff to help with a presentation, or he may have to accompany a wavering committee member to ask for a donation at the end of a meeting with a particular donor.

Another vital key to the whole process is to secure that first major gift, which will then stand out as a target for others and a signal that the appeal is likely both to succeed and to attract the right level of giving.

Gift aid

Do not forget that under the Gift Aid tax concession scheme, companies and individuals who pay tax can now effectively give sums over £250 to charities. Gift Aid lets the charity claim back the standard rate tax from the Government. Higher rate taxpayers can claim the extra 15% back for themselves through their tax returns. Forms are available from the Inland Revenue Claims Branch, St John's House, Merton Road, Bootle L69 9BB (R240 SD for Companies and R190 SD for individuals). You must use these forms. For individuals, it is fortunate that you can submit the form after the donations have been made! Remember that for companies, Gift Aid forms cannot be used if the company has paid via its charitable trust or via the CAF (Charities Aid Foundation). Booklet IR 112 explains the scheme in detail.

Reaching your target

- It helps if committee members have a breakdown of the number of gifts needed at several different amount levels, so that the potential donors' giving ability can be matched to one of those amounts. (Resist the temptation to let your committee members go for all the smaller sums.)

- Sometimes, if you cannot reach a good estimate of how much someone will be prepared to give, you can have three sums in mind and say something on the lines of, 'We are looking for two people who can give £X, four who can give half that amount, and six who will give a quarter of it. Would you care to join any of those groups?'

- Knowing how much to ask for, and actually asking for it, is crucial. If you are seeking to raise £1m you will probably need one donation of £250,000, two of £100,000, four of £50,000, and so on. Obviously, the key amounts are £250,000 and £100,000 and these should be raised first, or the appeal may flounder. If you can raise one gift of £500,000 this will make life a very great deal easier. Start with obtaining the top gift and work your way down.

- Researching into known supporters and their contacts is the key to finding that gift. Once the names of your most affluent supporters are known, research them carefully. You will often find that they have access to all sorts of opportunities that could help your organisation at a later date. (Gifts in kind from companies are an obvious idea. It is much easier for companies to give products, or unwanted fixtures or fittings, than cash, but this is not a substitute for appeal income.) Contacts with trustees of charitable trusts that could help are very useful, as is access to celebrities and decision makers. Working through your supporters on the basis of who knows whom is much more effective than making a direct approach from the outside.

I have undertaken this same process in India with a group of local industrialists who were keen to raise funds in their country for local projects - in this case, helping the poor improve their very small businesses (micro-enterprises), which had previously only been supported by European and Australian organisations.

WHEN YOU COME BACK AS A WHALE, YOU'LL BE BLOODY GLAD YOU PUT GREENPEACE IN YOUR WILL.

Help create a legacy for life on earth.

☐ Send me details of how to include Greenpeace in
☐ I'd like to join Greenpeace now.
☐ £14.50 Single ☐ £19.50 Family/Household ☐ Other do
☐ I enclose cheque/PO for £ _____ payable to
☐ Please charge my Visa/Access a/c no.

Signatory _____ Exp. date _____
Name: Mr/Mrs/Miss/Ms _____
Address _____
_____ Postcode _____

Please return to: **Greenpeace** FREEPOST, ND 944, Nor

GREENPEACE

Write her future into your will

Her future isn't hopeless. It will be difficult, certainly. But with Oxfam's help in her community, she intends to succeed in breaking the chains of poverty which held her parents captive all their lives.

Your legacy to Oxfam will make sure hardworking people all around the world achieve the independence their efforts deserve. When you're next changing ...'re making a new one – please ... by including Oxfam. And, if you can, ... done so, it really helps us plan for ... ll in the coupon, or call:

...65 312166

...mber Oxfam

...e provision for Oxfam in my will

...Miss _____

_____ Post Code _____

...on will be treated in the ...dence. Please post to:

OXFAM
Reg Charity No 202818

How would y_o_u like to be remembered?

As we pay tribute to those who died defending our peace, how will _our_ generation be remembered by young people of today?

Will the things _we_ believe in and support now, still be important in years to come?

The sad fact is that _two out of every three_ people who die today are remembered in a way they would never want to be - and by the very people they cared about most in life.

That is because they fail to make a Will, leaving their families to face an uncertain future.

Be remembered for all the right reasons

Whether you have already made a Will, or have yet to make one, you can find out how to be remembered for all the right reasons, by returning the coupon below today to: David Noble at the British Red Cross, Freepost, LONDON, SW1X 7BR.

Please tell me how I can be remembered for all the right reasons

NAME _____

ADDRESS _____
_____

_____ POSTCODE _____

Please tick the relevant box below to ensure we send you the right information. Thank you

I have already made a Will ☐   I have yet to make a Will ☐

Please send this completed coupon to David Noble, Planned Giving Manager, British Red Cross, Freepost, LONDON, SW1X 7BR.

Or you can telephone us on 071-201 5044.

British Red Cross
Caring for people in crisis

Registered Charity No. 220949   LPA 8

Fig. 4e *Take care to choose the style of legacy advertisement that suits your supporters.*

The hardest part was finding the chairperson, but it did not take long to come up with an extensive prospect list. Names from this list were allocated to those who knew them - naturally, this was usually the person who had put forward those names.

Legacies

Charities have been at the forefront in persuading the British public to make out a will and to leave part of their legacy to a good cause, but still less than half of us take that simple step.

As Britain has become increasingly a property owning nation, legacies have become big business. The sale of houses often releases much larger sums than their occupants ever disposed of in their lifetimes. Without a will the proceeds may not be used in the way they might wish.

Legacies are a potentially huge source of income, and no charity should be without a proactive legacy programme. CAF reports legacies amount to 33% of voluntary income to the top charities in 1993 but Smee & Ford show only 13.7% of people made a charitable will in 1994!

Key to success

The key to successful legacy work is to let your supporters understand that a percentage of the residue of an estate is your preference, rather than a set amount of money (which may be greatly reduced in value by inflation), and means that the legacies you receive will be some ten times greater in value than if you were left a simple lump sum.

Although we tend to talk of supporters in this context, some research has shown that perhaps half the legacies received by charities come from people who had not previously made a donation or become supporters or members. Taking this into account, most large legacy programmes feature advertising to the general public, often in the national press, usually offering free legacy advice in the form of a booklet. Naturally, charities hope that those who receive the booklet will leave them a proportion of the residue of the estate.

It is frequently said that these campaigns have been very successful, but they are certainly not run with the intensity that they were in the late Eighties, and I suspect that it is rather difficult to prove a connection between income and expenditure. This income is, however, not as tardy as one might suppose. The average time between the making of a will (or addition of a codicil) and the charity's receipt of the legacy is reliably quoted as being only three and a half years. The current trends may have altered this statistic a little, but it is still a surprisingly short time.

In planning your campaigns for legacies, bear the following points in mind:

* The seasons for making wills are in spring, before the family flies abroad for the summer holidays, and just before winter, when people fear the approaching cold.

- Most people seek legal advice on legacies, and you should always encourage your supporters to do this.

- The principal person people turn to when they are thinking of making a will is their solicitor, bank manager or other financial adviser. For that reason many charities advertise in the Solicitors' Journal and the Law Society Gazette. Many solicitors have told me they use these publications, but there is also a plethora of others designed especially for charities advertising for legacies. I suspect that, with so much money coming into charities via legacies, and so little direct feedback from such advertising, many charities simply advertise anywhere they can.

You need, as always, to test the market. The secret is to have an incentivised return coupon: 'Yes, I would like to receive a copy of your free Will guide'; 'Yes, I have left a legacy to you in my will. Please enter my name in your record of Lifetime Key Supporters, plant a tree in Charity Wood and send me that engraved fountain pen'. These things sound trivial, listed like that, but they are a real indication of a major decision and act of charity, which you should show you appreciate. You cannot thank someone after you have received the legacy. Of course, working out what percentage return from these coupons makes the expenditure worthwhile is not easy, but a comparatively low return may indicate there is some money to be saved on costs.

Legacy leaflets and advertising

To reach your supporters, a legacy leaflet is standard fare. This often goes to all members as an insert in the newsletter and then to all new members in your new member's pack.

- Consult your charity's legal adviser about the current state of taxation and legacies.

- Incentivise the return coupon.

- Set out sample wording for a will to help people to see how straightforward this can be, but make sure you also make it clear that standard wording will not suit everyone.

- Advise people to consult their solicitor before writing their will. It is very easy to make a simple mistake in will-writing and so fail to achieve what you set out to do. You may have solicitors who are supporters of your charity and could offer an advisory service to members.

- Include a list of the times in life to consider making a will or adjusting a previous will can set dates for people to get down to the task. At marriage, for example, previous wills are no longer valid. Other dates include:
  - buying a home
  - the birth of your children
  - divorce

- retirement
- the birth of grandchildren
- the death of family or friends
- receipt of a windfall or inheritance
- taking up a dangerous job or hobby
- planning your estate and tax position.

But it is the drip-feed approach that works in the long run. To achieve this you need to advertise in a small but readable way in each newsletter, then occasionally in any other publication you produce. That way your supporters become accustomed to the fact that legacies can be left to you, and their memories are also jogged on occasion, so that when the time comes to make out their will they cannot forget that you are interested.

Fig. 4f *Legacy leaflets are a good way of delivering detailed information at the right time.*

Some people worry about the effect a legacy programme may have on their older supporters, but the thought of death is not necessarily a problem for old people. They have had a lifetime to get used to the subject, and you need not be shy about writing about legacies and wills. If you do encourage someone to make out a will you have done them and their family a favour.

Visiting officers

The most progressive organisations now employ visiting officers, who contact their older members and offer to undertake any light services that they can provide, like shopping, or just calling in for a chat. This help is frequently deeply appreciated by older people, who are increasingly living on their own without an extended family to help them, and who may have contributed considerable sums to the charity when they were working. Naturally, this is no time for a hard sell, and any decision to leave money in a will must be taken spontaneously, but it can be a very rewarding process for all those who take part. Local group members often make lasting and valuable friendships with national supporters, and vice versa.

Another team activity is visiting solicitors and bank managers to mention that your charity can receive legacies and to leave leaflets and posters. A small volunteer team (best composed of retired solicitors and bank managers!) gradually covering the country in this way has proved invaluable to several organisations, including Oxfam.

One service you should definitely subscribe to is that run by: Smee and Ford, 2nd Floor, St George's House, 195/203 Waterloo Road, London SE1 8XJ, Tel: 0171 928 4050 WWW URL http://ourworld.compuserve.com/homepages/smee/

They will let you know the details of any legacy left to your charity and any open legacy, where it is left up to the trustees to decide which charity shall benefit. This is a potential goldmine, though in practice charities have had very mixed success.

Raffles

Like their gentleman-burglar namesake, raffles (though run within the law - in this case the Lotteries and Amusements Act of 1976) are fun and make a huge profit.

They can take place perhaps twice a year when books of, say, twenty 50p raffle tickets are mailed to each member and, say, ten books to each local group and other amounts to significant support groups. For an organisation of 100,000 members these tickets typically cost around £16,000 and bring in some £100,000 each time. It is possible to become very sophisticated in allocating additional books of tickets to those keen on selling them, and so run additional raffles throughout the year, but you must make sure that the complexity of this does not outweigh the benefits. Some people object to receiving raffle tickets on the grounds of waste, or on religious or moral grounds. It should be possible to flag these people on your database and to refrain from sending them further tickets.

The rules on raffles

- If you anticipate ticket sales of over £10,000 or the prizes are worth more than £2,000 you should register with the Gaming Board as well as your local authority, who can give advice about your legal position.

- If your tickets' value is under £10,000 and the prizes are worth no more than £2,000 you should register only with the Local Authority.

- Small lotteries, where prizes are less than £50 or have been donated during an event or entertainment, do not count as trading and do not need to be registered. Neither do private lotteries with tickets selling only to members of a club or society or people working together in the same place.

Fig. 4g *Even raffle tickets can help create synergy. Keep your campaigns and fundraising in step and they will both gain.*

An attractive cover on your raffle tickets will help them sell.

- You need to retain all raffle stubs for a period of four years after the raffle, unless you are given special exemption. This is to ensure a traceable audit trail.

- The name and address of your registered promoter must appear on the tickets.

The tickets

Send a book of raffle tickets to each member. This is usually done with the newsletter, to save postage. Tickets can be sold individually for 25p or 50p, and a book often holds £5 or £10 worth of tickets. Many members will just buy the whole book, so it does not pay to have books with less than £5 worth of tickets in them. It is well worth testing the selling capacity of your local groups and other associated bodies by sending them several books of tickets.

All tickets should be the same, though, of course, the serial numbers will differ, and none should have a greater chance of winning than any other.

List the range of numbers that go to each segment of your supporter base to check response, but if you sell many tickets, this can be very time consuming.

It is a good idea to have an attractive cover on a book of tickets and link it to one of your campaigns. You should also give enthusiastic sellers the chance to order more books by putting a form on the back of the cover, but if you do so, be sure to fulfil the order promptly.

The prizes

The key to successful raffles is their first prize. Often this is a holiday for two. For most people that is a problem. (Who do I go with? Can I get time off work? Will my husband want to go there? Can I afford the air fare, or the hotel at the other end?) You will find a cash first prize of, say, £1,000 works much better. It raises no problems in the buyer's mind, as it can be used to fulfil various needs.

Of course, the amount given in prizes must relate to the number of people likely to purchase tickets, and for some smaller organisations a £1,000 first prize would exceed the likely income.

The rest of the prizes should be as good as possible, though they are very much secondary items. These can be donated by friendly local firms or your suppliers, but it will take a personable and persistent individual a lot of time on the phone to obtain these goods. Your own trading goods can be used - but do not overvalue them. They are most likely going to people outside the organisation, so own-branded items will not have the appeal they do for your ardent supporters.

Ten prizes are quite adequate, but some organisations like to have a hundred or more. The main problem with this is that they take hours to draw - particularly when the celebrity insists on rummaging around to find tickets from the bottom of your huge tombola.

The draw

- Do look for a meaningful date to hold the draw of winning tickets, and seek out a celebrity or interesting person to do the draw. If you have a lot of prizes, check that the celebrity has time to draw them all.
- The tickets should be thoroughly mixed before the draw.
- Make sure the celebrity cannot see the tickets, and draws them out one by one.
- Photograph the draw and publicise it in your newsletter, along with a list of the winners. Many people will be convinced that they are going to win, and quite surprised if they do not. Seeing the draw and list of names will help show the draw was fair.

Notifying the winners

Let the winners know immediately and post the prizes off straight away. You will have phone calls on the day of the draw from people sure they have won, and you should let them know who the real prize winners are.

Publicising the list of winners takes up newsletter space and time, but it is essential to publicise the raffle, and such publicity also helps to show that it was operated fairly .

Recording names and addresses

It may seem a good idea to collect from your ticket stubs the names and addresses of all the people who bought raffle tickets, or have a computer bureau data-capture them (i.e. put all the names and addresses on a computer), and send them a letter asking them to join or donate. You would, however, be mailing people who like to buy raffle tickets, rather than people who like your organisation enough to join - though a test is well worth carrying out.

Be most careful that you use a very sophisticated de-duplication system, because you will be mailing many of your existing members, and they will write their names and addresses in a different way on each of the tickets they buy.

Be prepared for some surprises. People buy tickets for babies, putting their name and address on the stub. One supporter bought a ticket for his dog. I asked the dog to join. He joined. He was asked for a further donation. He was a very generous dog. He even filled in a member-gets-member list of his friends: Rover, Princess, etc...

Fundraising appeals and issue campaigning

A strong, well planned fundraising campaign will powerfully advance your organisation's issue campaigning. Often the money invested in generating new members and donors is far greater than that available for pure campaigning purposes. So it is natural for the organisation to look for a strong campaigning message to be used and this should 'fit' with your fundraising concepts.

The fundraising media are high-profile, e.g.:

- national press advertising, which, by its nature, is designed to have impact
- inserts in magazines which are read by thousands of people who, even if they do not join, will be positively influenced
- direct mail, which will also bring your message home to thousands of people.

All the techniques used in these media are intended to generate a response, and so will have been designed and written to be easily accessible and persuasive. The fact that their power is measurable (via the response coupon) means that you know the message is being put over correctly.

Pure campaigning rarely has such a self-correcting mechanism, and so it is hard to tell how effective it is and to alter it if it is not performing as well as expected. Naturally, some campaigning has goals which can clearly be seen to be met, e.g. by the passing of an Act of Parliament - but without a response device in your letters it may not be until the actual vote that your organisation has an inkling of how effective it has been.

Having said that, the justification of your budget is the financial return it will bring. So that is the prime purpose, and decisions on copy, choice of media, etc., must be taken primarily on fundraising grounds within the overall guidelines of the organisation.

Achieving synergy

It is important that fundraising and campaigning go hand in hand through the year to gain the maximum synergy. If your next campaign is on acid rain it is foolish for your next appeal to be on the ozone layer - unless the campaign is a deliberate attempt to include an unpopular subject in the year's work, and the ozone layer happens to be everyone's deep concern at the time the appeal is going out.

Bringing advocacy (campaigning action) and fundraising closer together also helps to build bridges with other departments, staff and committees. If you are seen to campaign, actively and effectively, it will help to create the recognition that fundraising has a powerful role to play at the heart of the organisation.

Taking advantage of the media

Your work will fare much better if, in general, you deal with topics that are featured in the media, especially television, rather than those your organisation particularly wants to highlight in order to change public perceptions. In responding to fundraising literature, members and donors often behave in a very similar fashion to the general public, which reacts to television as if it was the real world and is grateful for the opportunity to help alleviate any dreadful situation that is presented. One TV programme, however, is rarely enough to ensure this. The news itself is much more powerful, but this can be influenced by programmes like the compelling documentaries that themselves become news and so spill over into the rest of the media.

How effective is advocacy?

Asking the recipient of a fundraising appeal to undertake an act of advocacy often enhances the response, but it needs split testing to see if your organisation's advocacy methods have this result. You ignore split testing at your peril, and the first time you try mixing advocacy and appeals you might get the formula wrong - so

- test just 10% of your list (not 50%, as is common)
- if you can, test several variations, both of technique and of tone, at the same time. You could, for example, test five different approaches using 10% of your list for each one. This is best done after you know the basic concept is sound.

Linking advocacy with response to an appeal

You must link the act of advocacy with response to an appeal. If you are asking someone to write a letter, they should be asked to use words such as 'I have today joined/made a donation to X Charitable Trust'. Use approaches like, 'Please make a donation and then send our card to your MP. Tick the box on the return form and fill in your MP's name so that we know how many have been posted and to whom' can work well, both for your income and your campaigns.

What can go wrong

This whole process can, however, misfire badly. If it is not absolutely clear that what you really want, more than anything else, is money, then people will not bother to send it. They will see a campaigning letter, and may campaign or not, but they will rarely respond to a call for money that appears to be just tagged on. It is vitally necessary to make it clear just how important additional funds are to your work.

§

This process of upgrading supporters by moving them gradually up the steps of the fundraising pyramid can be deeply satisfying as your organisation's income grows but relationship fundraising teaches us that there is much more to long-term profitability than that. The more you can research and understand the needs of your supporters and then meet those needs on an individual basis the stronger the bond will be between you. The stronger the bond, the more satisfying and long-term that relationship will be.

5 Trading

Can charities trade?

Trading is not in itself a charitable object but charities can charge people and indulge in what is termed 'occasional fundraising activities' without infringing their charitable status or incurring a tax penalty from the Inland Revenue (trade is usually taxed at Corporation Tax rates). Trading must only be done occasionally, not regularly, and it must not be in competition with other traders. The public must be buying the goods because they wish to help the charity, and, of course, the profits must be used for the charity's charitable purposes. This is made clear in Inland Revenue leaflet C5.

If trading becomes (or looks like becoming) substantial or regular, then it is best to set up a limited company which covenants all of its profits to your charity. Instead of covenanting (which must be for four years or more), the company could use the Gift Aid scheme to remit funds tax effectively to your charity. If you need to retain profits for future expansion, you will probably be liable to corporation tax like any other company. The Inland Revenue leaflet IR75 deals with the rapid reclaiming of that tax by the charity. Because the company is limited, any losses it makes will not have to be met by the charity. Indeed, the charity could be in default of its objectives if it attempted to rectify the situation.

Inland Revenue permission is also needed for any loans made to the trading company at its outset or later. Repayment of these loans needs careful consideration, as all profits may have been covenanted back to the charity already!

It is prudent, as always, to seek legal advice in the setting up and running of a trading operation of this kind. An accountant's advice would also be helpful in making sure that the two legal entities are entirely separate. The accounts must be separate, and if there are shared staff and premises, it must be clear which part of the staffs' time and what proportion of space and overheads the trading operation will incur. The distinction between the two organisations must be quite clear at all times, and the charity cannot use the trading company to undertake activities on its behalf that it would not normally be allowed to do.

Interestingly, trade can be carried out by the charity if it directly helps the charity's charitable purposes, e.g. disabled people running shops or manufacturing units as part of their training and rehabilitation.

The contract culture

Unfortunately, governments are looking to charities and other voluntary bodies to take up their shortfall in social service provision. They are also harnessing charities and other NGOs to fit their policies and accountability by increasingly contracting out services to them and decreasing straightforward grant funding.

If these contracts are to provide services in the course of fulfilling charitable objectives, they are not trading and can even charge at a rate high enough to cover overheads and set aside reasonable provision for the future. Independent schools and private hospitals are both examples of charities that do not shrink from charging a good rate. Of course, at some stage, the amount charged will begin to interfere with the concept of benefiting the public. But remember that you do need to cover all your overheads, not just the running costs, or your organisation will be out of pocket. This includes the costs of monitoring and evaluating the services you provide, as well as the management time used in liaison and negotiation.

Do make sure that you have good legal advice that covers all aspects of your contracted services, grants and trading. An area that is coming under increasing scrutiny from the VAT inspectors and the taxperson, is that of the incentives given by charities in exchange for covenants or Gift Aid. The nominal value should not be more than 2.5% of the gift and there is a ceiling of £250, but magazines and other incentives can be deemed to have a much higher value than their production costs. Be careful of the cover price on your magazine or newsletter and the value of other incentives. If in doubt, check before you launch a costly scheme that might incur tax and VAT on the whole of the gifts raised.

The key to successfully managing the contract culture is to ensure that your income strategy covers the long term and allows for major funders to drop out and others to replace them. Do not become over dependent on one source of income, and keep trawling the market for new areas of funding.

Catalogues

Your membership forms a niche market of a certain kind of person. One thing is sure: they like your organisation and probably wish to be associated with it. The Henley Centre for Forecasting, among others, has highlighted the phenomenon that people are increasingly defining themselves in terms of the organisations they support and their profession, rather than the place they come from. They are, for example, beginning to think of themselves as members of the World Wide Fund for Nature rather than inhabitants of Tottenham.

This enhances the possibility of selling them goods which bear your logo, even T-shirts which make abundantly clear the wearer's allegiance. Naturally, you will need to discover what kinds of goods interest your supporters. In this respect organisations like the RSPB have an easy task. It is not difficult to think of the products their members will purchase. If you look at a few catalogues it will become obvious that there are several items that most organisations can market, such as T-shirts, tea-towels, re-use labels and Christmas cards.

Trading will add synergy by cementing loyalty, spreading your message, giving an easy way for everyone to assist financially, and helping your local groups earn funds and reach the public.

Starting out

If you are starting out to create a new catalogue, begin with the items mentioned above.

- Choose the best designer you can find, and use only good quality materials. (Art colleges can be helpful, but you must direct students carefully and be firm with sub-standard work.) If you produce shoddy goods it will reflect badly on your work and you will not be able to build up repeat purchases, which are the foundation of your future sales.

- Budget, taking into account a certain proportion of your stock will not sell. Write down some stock, and then allow for 'shrinkage'.

- Do not drop old favourites that are selling well but change the designs slightly to keep them up to date.

- Only buy for one catalogue at a time, to keep stocks down. If you can order small quantities repeatedly and still have them arrive in time (without costing more because of the small manufacturing run), this will also help to keep the stock cost down. This is important as money held in stock cannot be used for anything else and is a waste. Aim for 'just in time' delivery.

- Start small with a few items until you know the kinds of goods your supporters will buy. Do not be afraid to charge a premium for branded items - you have an exclusive item! The usual mark-up is around 2.5 times the purchase price.

Setting out the catalogue

There are many commercial books about catalogue layout, and their wisdom applies to charities as much as commercial firms.

- The cover sets the tone of the catalogue. You can use it to increase sales of your best items and attract people inside with a picture of something you know they will like. Put your best-selling items on the cover, not those you are trying to shift.

- Use the first pages to talk to your customers, setting out your policy and philosophy of trading. Let them know you care about your customers. A

Fig. 5a *Why let your supporters buy from anywhere else ? They will pay more for a T-shirt from you because they gain the "benefit" of supporting and being associated with their favourite charity as well as a T-shirt.*

celebrity endorsement helps so long as it actually encourages people to buy rather than just saying that your charity is a worthy cause. It is quite acceptable to draft this letter for the celebrity and to allow them to add a personal note or change something if they wish. Some will rewrite your draft improving it greatly, others will just sign the draft.

• Use colour, because your customers' main worry will be whether the product matches other items they have, etc. Do not just use a picture and leave it at that, but mention key points and important details. A simple, clear layout can still show a lot of items per page, but do make sure they are clearly visible. Your customers will want to see exactly what they are buying, because they cannot call in at a shop and see the goods first.

• People are buying the benefit of having your product, not the product itself. Describe products in those terms, and your sales will increase.

• Make sure you have priced, numbered and described the items accurately.

• Keep a fair turnover of goods by marking down and selling off slow-moving items, but do not let them clog up your catalogue. Keep it looking fresh and interesting. (Use local groups to sell off goods cheaply rather than letting them take up valuable selling space in your catalogue).

• Try out what everybody else does. They may be doing it because it works!
    - Send out your catalogue a long time before Christmas and mention it in your next newsletter.
    - Try two issues with the same contents but different covers.
    - Do not try a spring catalogue until you have established your Christmas market.
    - Use celebrity endorsements. They sell products and add glamour to your organisation.
    - Provide a clear and simple order form, and a FREEPOST address to save people finding an envelope and stamp.

Insert your catalogue in your newsletter to save postage and avoid clashing with your appeals - but test to see if a separate mailing may not be more profitable.

Giving good service

Complaints will usually come from activists who believe the products should be cheap and the catalogue printed on poor quality paper. The compliments will come from repeat orders by your national members who appreciate receiving exactly what they saw, on time. This is especially true before Christmas.

• It is absolutely essential to have adequate stocks ready to send out on time. Let people know the last date for ordering. If items they have bought as gifts do not arrive in time for them to send on to friends they will not give you a second chance.

- Apologise and explain promptly if you have any problems in supplying goods.
- Make it really easy for people to buy from you and to return the goods if they are not happy.
- Refund money quickly if you have to.

Market research

Survey your buyers and your non-buyers: learn everything you can about them.

- Why didn't they buy anything? (Perhaps your catalogue distribution was not as efficient as you thought it was. Perhaps your goods are too old fashioned, or too trendy, for your members. Are they to your taste or theirs?)
- Are they buying for themselves or to give to others?
- What would your members like to see in the catalogue?
- What have they bought from your competitors' catalogues recently?
- Are your buyers men or women ? Is there an obvious reason for that?

   Act on the information you receive, and do not ask a question unless you know that you can use the answer.

Increasing turnover

- Send a second catalogue and order form to anyone who buys anything. Give them an opportunity to pass the catalogue on to a friend, and give that friend an opportunity to join or donate to your organisation.
- Allow the purchaser to use as many means of paying as possible - e.g. credit cards, cheques and postal orders. Establish a credit card hotline and make sure it is properly maintained.
- Your order form should also give the opportunity to round up the purchase price with a donation.

Going outside the membership

- Test your catalogue, or a version of it, in the magazines that your members read.
- Try a loose-leaf insert with a FREEPOST coupon to return, requesting a copy of your catalogue.
- Code all these inserts so that you can check which magazines worked best, and code each catalogue you send out likewise, so that you know exactly in which market it has been cost-effective.

Sometimes you can be highly successful by ignoring the conventional wisdom. Lynx was very successful in taking full-page colour ads selling their T-shirts. The WWF was very successful in creating a catalogue that appealed to a very wide range of people outside their list of supporters, enabling them to build up a separate list of purchasers hundreds-of-thousands strong. They also used a smaller version of their catalogue to send to each purchaser and, on a reciprocal basis, to send to the purchasers of other organisations' catalogues. That way a huge database of catalogue-friendly people can be built up. Of course, you will need to have a well-established catalogue with a large enough range of excellent products that appeal to a wide audience in order to achieve this.

There are commercial mail order companies which cater for charities by providing a goods, dispatch and fulfilment service. These can save you a great deal of time and effort if their kind of goods match your supporters taste. Make sure the products offered fit with the expectations your supporters have of your organisation, both for quality and for their likely needs.

Licensing

Licensing well-known trademarks

Licensing deals for charities have their origins in the licensing of well-known trademarks such as cartoon characters, cinema and TV heroes. Suitable products would be designed by a design company and sold on to a manufacturer who would manufacture the goods and in turn sell the goods on to their usual outlets, or would perhaps find new outlets for such goods. A star like Mickey Mouse would then appear on a bewilderingly large variety of products, from straightforward toys to curtains and bedspreads, as well as coat hooks and torches. A licensing agent would take the copyright owner through the whole process putting the best deal forward, looking after their clients' interests and maximising their return.

Several charities have gone down this route, with varying degrees of success. World-wide sales of many quite different products can be achieved in ways that an individual charity would never be able to think of, let alone manage making the contacts and developing the organisation necessary. It only really works, however, for key trademarks that are well known, highly respected, and capable of translation into goods people wish to buy. It is, for example, a lot easier for a well known environmental organisation to market soft toy animals than for a charity looking after the homeless to find a suitable product or product range. A great deal of time and energy can be consumed in trying to design appropriate products that do not sell on. If an agent's fees are clocking up at the same time a charity can rapidly find itself making a heavy loss.

Licensing products

Some catalogues feature unique or popular products that have a well-known household name, to which a suitable segment of the market will respond. Amnesty has licensing deals with manufacturers of stationery, calendars, greetings cards and other such items. These feature the positive side of

Amnesty's work in pictures about freedom, the candle logo, doves and other appropriate symbols. The calendar pictures are the sort one could wish to see on one's wall, though each has some text about the human rights violations that take place in any countries featured.

At this level it is a matter of negotiating directly with a manufacturer. Often this will be someone you already know, who creates a similar product to those in your catalogue. It is often very difficult to make the first deal. Manufacturers find it hard to imagine a product from a not-for-profit charity, but once one commercial product is in the shops it suddenly appears feasible. The fears that dealing with a charity is a nightmare, or that the public will never buy something associated with torture or vagrants, or whatever, quickly fade - especially if sales are high.

You will find that one of the most difficult questions is the extent to which the charity should benefit. Some organisations get over this by saying that they want a certain percentage and a guarantee of £5,000 per year for each product on which their logo is featured. Others demand 10% of the sales price regardless of the market or costs. Others will look at sales each year and negotiate new rates; but it is very hard to do this if you have started too low or are unsure about the producer's profits.

The pitfalls

One thing is certain. You must never allow your logo to be used on products without receiving a financial return.

- Many apparently altruistic companies will try to tell you they are doing you a great favour by featuring your logo on their products. Do not fall for this, and be quite prepared for the deal to fail if no money is forthcoming.

- Make sure you do not accept anything less than a reasonable percentage of the sales price (or of profits if you are going to receive strict accounting informing you in clear language how much the profit is).

- Sometimes you can simply place your address or phone number on a product. Usually, this will merely result in nuisance calls and is not worth serious consideration. People do not usually join organisations through products. Of course, if you need people to call for a specific reason this can be a way to reach the public.

Working with commercial retailers

If you are dealing with an external chain of commercially-run shops, a wider deal is quite possible.

- Window space backed up by leaflets (with coupons!) and a counter can for donations can be quite effective. Tread very warily with lesser deals. Leaflets on display are fine.

- Posters in the shops with your name on are probably not much use to you unless you are a local charity and need that sort of publicity.

The type of work you do and the publicity you need will condition your response to these sorts of offers. It may be very effective for your local groups to be able to work with a chain of shops because they have a high street presence, a meeting room, or a management with particular expertise your groups may lack.

It is also well worthwhile to think about the long term. If you are too demanding on day one you may not get a look in on day two, or year two or three. It's all a question of judgement, but negotiating is a two-way process in which both organisations benefit, even if one needs to demonstrate publicly that one is the benefactor (and the other the recipient) of favours.

Local group trading

A local group has an entirely different market from a national headquarters. The group is usually selling goods at events, to passers-by who will linger by a stall and purchase a few items whilst they chat to the stall holder. Another key source of income for local groups is their membership, and their trading officer and/or fundraiser should start by making sure that all group members are aware of the range of goods on offer, and have bought all they wish to.

What to sell

The goods that sell best are relatively low-value items, small and conventional. They are the sort of thing that someone will buy anyway, and can purchase without fear of making a mistake:

- greetings cards
- simple, informative publications about the organisation
- goods with the organisation's logo on, such as
  - re-use labels
  - biros
  - stickers
  - badges, etc.

The small outlay needed is often readily available to a local group and the income is useful for its running expenses. An organisation providing such goods will help its local groups a great deal.

At a slightly more ambitious level

- a range of attractive T-shirts
- stationery items
- mugs
- Christmas cards

can greatly improve a local group's income. The key word here is 'attractive'. You will only persuade your groups to buy (and a great many organisations have lost large amounts of money through sale-or-return) if the goods are really well designed and people will be pleased to wear them or have them in their homes.

Trading goods are not hard campaigning devices. 'I support X hospital' is fine, and people will be happy for others to see that they support X. 'Sack the Health Minister' is an aggressive statement that few will wear on their chests or want on their coffee mugs. Of course, you must judge your particular public carefully. What sort of designs do appeal to them? Perhaps they like attractive pictures of mountains or rare breeds of animals, but they may also like hard or cheeky slogans.

Where and when to sell

Goods should, of course, be sold every time the group meets the public and there is room to display the goods. Often the mere fact that the group has goods for sale will enable it to mount a satisfactory presence at many local events. Especially valuable are those that the whole locality seems to turn out for, such as pre-Christmas sales and Easter Fayres. There may be many similar stalls, but there will also be customers who are in the mood to browse, chat and buy as they circulate.

If the group is confident enough it can usually make more money by renting a local hall and hiring out the space it does not need to other organisations for a special event. In this case, of course, there is ample opportunity for you to take the prime position for your own goods. It is wellworth while testing several different 'markets' before settling on the best place to sell your goods.

How to sell

1 Buy goods in sufficient quantities to earn a good discount, but not more than you can comfortably shift in the next six months.

2 If they do not sell, reduce the price to your purchase price and try again.

3 If they still do not sell, reduce the price to next to nothing to shift them.

As with catalogues, do not clog up your stall/selling space with unsaleable items. Keep the merchandise moving and avoid having the same old stuff on display every time, but do keep adequate stocks of good selling lines.

Maximise your successes, cut your losses and brighten up your image with new items. Shops often have interesting goods on display that will not sell particularly well, but which draw buyers into the shop because they are unusual or very attractive in some way. Your stall can benefit from these 'strange attractors', too.

Shops

Why shops?

Most NGOs depend, as we have seen, on their membership/donor-base for a very large part of their income. A few have significant sums from the government or trusts or from commercial companies, but these are not usually sources of sustainable long-term income. Shops

- offer a reliable way of diversifying your income which is probably subject to a different business cycle than your membership
- can be expanded across the country depending only on the amount you are willing to invest and the availability of prime site, high street premises. (Do not bother with anything less - you will not be seen by those giving or those buying.)

In recessionary times it is particularly easy to open charity shops because the institutional landlords who control most of our high streets are less choosy about who they rent to. Traditionally, they are opposed to charity shops 'lowering the tone' of their shopping parades and, by implication, the rentable value of their commercial properties.

The charity shop market looks saturated. Your high street may have a plethora of different charity shops, and they will tell you there is no point in opening another one; but you should be aware that customers tend to 'do the rounds' of charity shops and come quite long distances to check out a group of several charity shops.

Is a shop a good campaigning base?

If you have the choice of opening a shop for either your organisation's charitable or non-charitable wing you must consider whether it is important for you to use the shop as a campaigning base for your non-charitable activities, and whether your local group members will be likely to play an active role in the shop. If so, that role might need to be restricted. The experience of most charities is that their shop's customers are not interested in the cause, and leaflets rapidly gather dust.

This is not to say that the shop should be devoid of relation to the cause. The high street presence will act to make people aware of you, and your fascia and displays should reflect your name and work. This will, naturally, encourage donations of goods and remind your helpers why you are there.

Attracting the public

Though the British are deemed to be a nation of shopkeepers, sound commercial sense is often abandoned when charity shops are opened. If you follow the example of the smart, well-presented shops of the market leaders you will not do badly.

- In charity shops, appearances are everything. Like attracts like, and good quality attractive clothing attracts more of the same.
- Good quality clothing in attractive surroundings attracts customers who will pay the best prices.
- Helpful, friendly volunteers attract more of the same. (Unfortunately, the reverse is also true, with disastrous consequences for many charity shops.)
- An up-market location in a prime site is far better than a mid-range location - and poor locations should be completely avoided.

Quality control—clothing

Clothing is the mainstay of charity shops. The kind of customer who is used to buying expensive clothing is quite happy to tell the world about the designer label they bought for only a few pounds in a charity shop; but the poor will buy new, cheap, poor quality clothing and avoid at all costs appearing to have bought second-hand.

It is difficult to run a good-looking charity shop with a clutter of bric-a-brac and books, which hardly pay their keep. If you start selling junk you will have tons of it delivered the next day, and the day after that. Everyone has junk they would like to give to a good cause.

- Be absolutely ruthless in sorting through the things given to you.
- If you are keeping more than 20% you are not being ruthless enough and the quality of your goods will nosedive. Throw the rest away.
- Clothing can, however, be recycled through the Oxfam Wastesaver scheme by other charities.

Choosing premises

The location

Stage one, as usual, is defining your needs. If you have a choice of towns, start in the best location in the largest town and work your way down slowly.

- Undertake a pedestrian count outside your favoured locations to see which is doing the most business. Simply count the number of people passing on the same day of the week at the same time, and compare shop with shop.
- Check to make sure that there is vehicle access, ie. that people can draw up and unload easily and quickly close to the shop.
- Is there a high-class residential area around the shop to provide goods and customers?
- What are the rents and rates, and will they be reviewed in the near future? (If you are a charity you will be entitled to a 50% rate reduction but some councils will give you a 100% reduction. If you are not a charity but have philanthropic purposes you can still apply and may receive considerable relief.)

The shop

Once you have found a suitable area, you still need suitable premises.

- Look for a shop with adequate frontage so that people can find you and you can display your goods. Give yourself plenty of space to display goods.
- Remember, one third of the floor space will be needed to store, sort and price goods, as well as giving room for helpers to relax and have a break.
- Use a good surveyor and solicitor to make sure you know all about the condition of the premises and the conditions of the lease or sale (just who is responsible for the roof if there are several floors to the premises, etc.).

Before you open shop

Do not be in a rush to open. Give yourself more than enough time to do the following:

1 Fit the shop out properly.
2 Build up and train a team of volunteers to run the shop (including your shop leader who is by far the most important element in the shop and will ensure its success or otherwise).
3 Attract, process and display goods.

Fitting out the shop

Having an architect design the shop and give detailed instructions to the builders will save a lot of heartache later. Make sure you really approve of the design, and that it is based on the best models. Do not attempt to oversee the fitting out of the premises yourself if you have no experience. It may prove very costly dealing with builders and shop fitters. Make sure that you have taken health and safety issues into full consideration, including fire exits and that all legal requirements are covered.

Making the most of your space

Starting outside the shop

- The fascia board should be clearly painted so that customers and donors know exactly who you are.
- A hanging sign helps in a busy street (and if it's not busy you should not be there).
- The window and door should be clear, with no handwritten notices. (Neither should there ever be any in any other part of the shop.)
- The two notices that should be clearly displayed are the opening times (with the open/closed sign) and the fact that you need good quality, clean clothing delivered during these times only.

Any window display should be clean, neat, attractive and regularly changed. The door should be open during shop hours with an overhead heater to keep the shop warm in winter. You will need a doormat to preserve the carpet.

Inside the shop

- The carpet should be cheap and strong in a neutral colour, with no pattern.
- Lighting should be good - a false ceiling may be needed if the roof is too high.
- Make a clear space to tell people about your charity, and keep the leaflets stocked and tidy.
- Maximum use should be made of the space without it being crowded: customers should be able to move freely around the shop even when it is quite busy.
  - Flexible fittings are a must, so that you can rearrange the shop at regular intervals and test different ideas.
  - The counter should be near the door (with an electronic till which can divide up the different kinds of items you sell so that you can test which are earning their keep in terms of square feet taken up).
  - Changing rooms are essential but should be as open as possible, because they are the area in which goods disappear. (Price tickets are often stuffed behind the mirrors in changing rooms, so have the mirrors fitted outside. Only allow one garment at a time, and try to have extra volunteers to supervise at busy times.)
- There should be a phone by the till, and in the back room (so that you can phone the police in case of need; they will often come if you are going to ask an awkward customer to leave).

The sorting room

The sorting room requires special attention, as that is where the money is made. To avoid having sorters bend over for long periods adequate worktop space is necessary, with industrial bins to hold black sacks for the discarded clothing and rails for that accepted, and shelves for books, so that the pricers can come along later and price up the goods.

- A safe area for valuables is essential, as is somewhere for volunteers to keep their bags, etc.
- Tea- and coffee-making facilities should be safe and easy to use.
- Toilets and washrooms must conform to regulations.

Sorting, labelling and pricing goods

- Discard everything that is torn, dirty or old-fashioned, and be absolutely ruthless in sorting.
- To assist pricing it helps to have a guide listing the suggested pricing for different kinds of clothing against the average retail prices.
- Make sure your pricers are genuinely interested in clothing, and let them look at several other charity shops to get the feel of current prices.

- The great fear of people giving quality items is that you will sell them too cheaply. People giving expensive goods like to be asked what they paid for them as it shows you are taking pricing seriously.
- Label and price everything. Nothing must go into the shop unpriced, or customers will bargain with the person on the till and force the price down. (They will also take the labels off anything else that is priced, and try to bargain for that as well.).Often they will pick on the mildest person in the shop late on Thursday night and beat them into giving designer clothes away for pennies: 'It's for my poor dog to sleep on!' I heard it said about a perfect silk dress.
- Make it a rule that if something has no price it is withdrawn from sale immediately (even if the ticket is discovered a few seconds later).
- All clothing should be date-coded and withdrawn from sale after about two weeks.

Displaying goods

- All clothing should be on plastic hangers, which you can easily obtain for free from commercial clothing shops as they receive new clothes on plastic hangers. Never use metal coat-hangers as they look dreadful and get tangled up like wild animals.
- Buy smart rails to display your clothing and do not allow dump bins to emerge in the shops.
- Shoes and underwear should not be sold. They are impossible to display well, and do not sell.
- Do not display anything you would not like to receive six of the next day. If you put out only antiques, you will receive only antiques. Bric-a-brac should be restricted to small items of good quality.
- Restrict the area available to books unless they are really selling well. Popular paperback fiction sells well but academic books rarely sell at all.
- Compare the sales per square foot of books, clothing and bric-a-brac and adjust your displays accordingly.

Recruiting volunteer staff

While fitting out is in progress, put in the window a notice with your phone number on it requesting volunteers, and begin to build up a weekly rota of staff. You must have at least two people in the shop at all times.

The first person you are looking for is the shop leader. They will make or break the shop. Usually, they are women who live locally, do not wish to work full-time and whose children have left home or are independent. They will enthuse the volunteers and bring in sensible, caring people to run the shop. That team will take time to settle in and there may be several changes of staff before the rota is really set, though after the first year there will probably be very few changes.

You will need to build up different teams to sort, repair and price goods. Each is a special skill and it takes time and practice to acquire the necessary experience, which is then invaluable.

Volunteers can come from a variety of sources. If you have a national membership or donor-base they can be telephoned or written to. You should advertise in the local press and put up cards in sweetshop windows. Each method will probably recruit only a few people, but that is all you need before the shop opens and begins to do its own recruiting.

Opening up shop

When everything is ready hold a grand opening day and advertise it widely.

- If you have any celebrities associated with your charity ask them to come, so that you feature in as many local papers as possible.

- Issue a press release before opening day, and afterwards let the press know how well it went.

- Try to arrange for interviews with the shop leader and any volunteers with appropriate and interesting stories to tell.

- Make sure that you have your own photographer to cover the event and send pictures to the press as their photographer will have many calls on a Saturday (which is the usual opening day).

Tips for good public relations

- Create good relationships with other local traders, the police and, especially, the refuse collectors.

- Make sure the back of the shop is clean and tidy. If you have unsavoury or bulky goods dumped on your premises take them quickly to the local dump to avoid more arriving.

Third World goods and new products

Oxfam is the market leader for selling 'third word' craft goods through shops, but beware! Oxfam's profits on these goods come from their catalogue sales to a steady market of subscribers. The goods in the shops are attractive and can sell well, but they do not bring the profits that the second-hand items attain. The cost is an internal pricing transfer and need not be the real market price.

Oxfam's policy is to support co-operatives until they find a commercial market for their goods, then to move on. Naturally, they cannot easily abandon co-operatives whose goods are not selling well. This is an ethical dilemma that those thinking of entering that market should consider carefully. The expense of overseas travel and working with co-operatives to ensure prompt delivery and quality control is very high. To import such goods, you will need very experienced buyers and delivery organisers. Many organisations have been caught with goods stuck in customs, months late or only bearing a passing resemblance to the sample first proffered.

Such trading goods do, however, provide an attractive appearance for the shops - particularly the window display and, in the right location, sell well.

It is possible to come to an understanding with manufacturers, to receive their ends-of-lines as the season changes. This can be very profitable but it cannot be relied upon for steady sales through the year. With just-in-time delivery, zero stocks, computerised warehousing and industrial retailing, the goods left unsold have been cut down to a fraction of those in former years. Of course, there is still that happy change of fashion in the high street which passes unnoticed outside the city centres.

§

Last but not least...

...shopkeeping is great fun, and many amusing incidents occur during the day. It is a good idea to have an incident book for helpers to record useful information and anecdotes. This not only serves as a friendly link between people who may never actually meet but also as a very practical one. For example, it can alert helpers to the latest scam by unscrupulous customers, or give the shop leader many good ideas for improvements.

6 Outside the Pyramid

There is, of course, a wide variety of fundraising techniques that fall outside the traditional fundraising pyramid. Instead of depending on known supporters you may look to the general public or try to secure funds from targeted individuals, trusts and foundations, companies or from government sources, etc. Of course, many of the people contributing through these techniques may also be members or donors and a donor-base is a fine place to start to seek an audience for events, a group of sympathetic trustees of charitable trusts, or a group of august but friendly company chairpersons.

Probably the most popular of these is the charity event. There are at least as many of these as there are charities - and that is a lot! You will find that successful events usually fall into one of two different categories. One is the sponsored event, in which hundreds of people undertake a walk, swim, parachute jump or some such collective activity and collect money from their friends, colleagues and relatives. The other is the kind of event that has an entrance fee, such as concerts and other performances, or where people gather to buy goods, such as village fetes and auctions.

Sponsored events

Sponsored events are good fundraisers for organisations with large membership or local group structures. If supported from the centre with materials, T-shirts and national publicity, the local groups can become very serious money makers.

Sponsored walks have long been the traditional sponsored activity, but

Fig. 6a *Stickers and other appropriate items help to promote events and enhance their attraction.*

charities have done very well out of sponsored swims, cycle rides, and a large variety of other activities. It helps if you can link up with an appropriate company or add a special flavour to the event. Some years ago Friends of the Earth organised a mass sponsored walk through London's parks, called Ark Day, in which participants, dressed as animals, walked to a huge ark built at the highest point of the city. Thousands of people took part in the spectacular event and enjoyed the day out. There is most likely a feature of your work that would help to raise a sponsored event out of the ordinary. I have seen local groups undertake long tractor pulls for the Young Farmers and bed-pushes for local hospitals.

The funds for sponsored events come from individuals asking their friends and colleagues face-to-face for money for a charity in which they believe. This is a very effective proposition. It is helped if the person asking has a well-designed form to fill in, showing just how the money raised will be used, and if they are enthusiastic and persistent. An incentive to raise a lot of money helps the person asking to say, 'Please give generously because I'm trying to raise the most money so that I can ...' and for the person giving to think, 'I'm being extremely generous this time because I want to help him/her to ...'

Keys to success

Incentives such as a T-shirt for each £50 raised, a jacket for £100 and an appropriate gift for £500, can make far more money than merely selling T-shirts to participants, and if you change the T-shirt design each year, people will collect them.

Your key to running a successful sponsored event is to maximise the number of people taking part and to ensure the first gift pledged on the sponsorship form is a large one, because everyone following will agree to give the same amount. You ensure this by simply printing in a sample sponsor and gift: John Brown, Anytown, £5... This looks best if done in half-tone.

Expeditions

Charities are often approached by individuals who wish to undertake a particularly difficult or hazardous task or trek, like climbing the Matterhorn or crossing the Sahara on a bicycle. These offers should be treated with extreme caution. They are well meant but show a fundamental lack of knowledge about how sponsored events work. It is very unlikely that people in your organisation, or their friends and colleagues, will give money because someone they probably do not know is undertaking a difficult task.

This is not to say that those expeditions do not have their contribution to make. This is really from the publicity that they can engender in the media for the cause. It will help all your other fundraising if someone is seen to be making such a huge effort to help. The sponsorship, in this case, comes from companies giving equipment that can be featured in any photographs or filming of the trek,

SPONSORSHIP FORM - PLEASE USE BLOCK CAPITALS

WALK FOR LIFE 95/96
REF: 322AB

AMNESTY INTERNATIONAL BRITISH SECTION

Please Sponsor (Name) .... (Group name where app.)

of (address) ....

....

.... Postcode ....

on their .... mile **Walk for Life** on (date) ....

SPONSORS ARE REQUESTED TO PAY THEIR CONTRIBUTIONS TO THE WALK FOR LIFE PARTICIPANT WITHIN ONE MONTH OF COMPLETION OF THEIR WALK FOR LIFE.
Please photocopy this form before filling in if you need more space for sponsors, or ring 0171-814-6200 for more forms

Sponsors Name (Block Capitals Please)	Address (including POSTCODE) + Telephone No.	Amount per mile	Total
Tony Morrison	15 Solomon St, Reba, CA4 1AA - 071-123-4567	5.00	10.00

Page sub total

Declaration

I have completed my .... mile AI "Walk for Life" and I promise to pay Amnesty International all monies pledged within 1 month of my Walk for Life.

Signed .... **Participant**

Complete box below for total payment only

Total Sponsor money enclosed

Important

Please make all cheques/postal orders payable to Amnesty International. Please do not send cash. Send your sponsor money **WITH THIS FORM** to Walk for Life, AIBS, 99-119 Rosebery Avenue, London EC1R 4RE

Tick if you would like a receipt ☐

Fig. 6b *Note the specimen amount already filled in - how much will the next person give?*

which the company can use for marketing purposes. Occasionally, the participants can raise quite significant sums themselves from affluent contacts, or sometimes from companies if what they are doing is certain to feature on a television programme. It is important that all this is made clear by your organisation from the start, otherwise the participants may feel badly let down by you, for failing to take full advantage of their hard work by not raising much money.

Planning a sponsored event

* Make sure the route goes from A to A, not A to B, or the participants will have a long journey back at the end of their efforts.
* Everyone who agrees to take part should have
  - a route map
  - clear instructions
  - a sponsorship form that can be photocopied.

It helps if the form has a space for telephone numbers because after the event those who take part will need to ring round all their sponsors and chase up the pledges quickly before they go cold.

* Your local organiser will need to know who has taken part in their area so that they can chase up the money likely to come in. It is the organiser's enthusiasm that will keep the event going from year to year and will enable it to become more and more successful.
* T-shirts to wear on the walk and photographs of participants to take home afterwards, help to make the event fun and unified. If people have endured certain hardships together they become closer, and these events can engender a spirit of camaraderie which helps them to continue year after year. (Don't lose participants' names and addresses.)
* It is usual to sign (stamp) people in at the beginning and out at the end, so showing that the course has been completed. (A certificate like this helps the pledges to be collected.)
* You will need enough marshals to cover the late starters and finishers, and along the route to help people over roads or with any difficulty they may have in following the route.
* Some drink and refreshment is very helpful during a very long walk.
* Always
  - notify the local police
  - check your insurance
  - take every precaution over safety to eliminate risks as far as possible.

Any open air event can be insured against rain. This is, however, very expensive, often one fifth of the amount insured. The time you are insuring for also needs careful thinking through. Do you simply insure against rain at the time the event takes place, or for, say, a two-hour period in the morning when people are making up their minds whether to attend, or on a Friday morning for a Saturday event?

Concerts and open air events

The second type of event is epitomised by the rock concert. Here artists forgo their fee (giving their time or art for free), and the proceeds from the event go to the charity.

Planning for a concert

The big surprise for most people is just how risky these events are. Especially serious are the artists' expenses. After the initial contact with a celebrity you will probably be dealing with their management and you can be sure that they don't care about your charity at all. In fact they will see you as a good chance to fly their star, the band and tons of equipment back from South America for free, as well as an opportunity to have two weeks in the best hotel in town for a large number of people they owe favours to.

Limit expenses, and read the contract details carefully. Most of them are designed to stop the artist being put into a squalid hotel, taxiing around at their own expense, and changing in sordid dressing-rooms - but does the carpet really have to be turquoise, and do they need that amount of root ginger before appearing on stage? Everything is negotiable, up to a point.

The entertainer's fee is only a small part of your expenses, so you are still left with major costs. You should consider

- hire of the hall
- advertising
- publicity
- programme printing
- sundry expenses (which can easily amount to more than the total take if not watched rigorously).

When drawing up your budget, allow 10% of the expected income for publicity and have another 10% contingency sum so that you can cover the unexpected. You may need this at the last minute to boost ticket sales. These will be much easier to judge after the first year.

Points to watch

- When approaching stars, ask the best first. (Who wants to join the worst on stage?)
- Making sure the artist and venue match is extremely important.

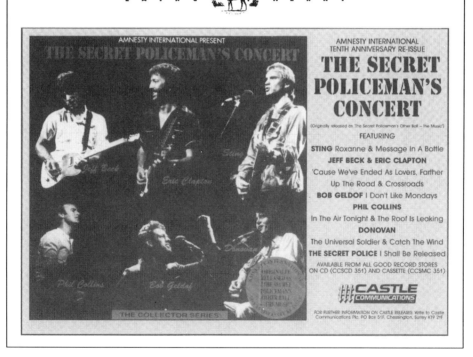

Fig. 6c *Many firms have a budget for charity advertising - and don't forget to ask all your commercial suppliers.*

- Check carefully that the artist has not just failed to fill a larger venue. If they have just toured, will their fans go yet again to see them? Read the music press to keep in touch if you are planning such an activity.

- If you have more than one artist appearing make sure they complement each other. Do not assume that if you have five completely different artists you will have five times the audience. People will not sit through a performance by someone they cannot stand in order to hear someone they like.

- You must only reveal the names of artists to the press when they have definitely agreed. This can take some time as their management will try to hold out for as long as possible in case paid work comes up.

- Fix a deadline to decide when all confirmations from performers must be in, and stick to it.

- You should spend enough on advertising to fill the venue, but budget to break even at half full and to be profitable at two-thirds full. It is surprising how often an event is two-thirds full and how often the real break-even point is a full venue.

- Straightforward promotional ideas are best. Free tickets or T-shirts to radio shows and newspapers for listeners and viewers who ring in first or who answer a simple quiz correctly are a very good investment, which gives your show integrity in the eyes of the audience (being linked to their favourite show) as well as publicity.

- Photo opportunity stunts are fun, but the chances are you will have to take your own photos and push them to the press (not forgetting to take your own broadcast-quality video for an electronic news release).

Events always take up twice the staff time you have available but are an excellent opportunity to make the most of your volunteer support. Draft in volunteers early, and give them specific tasks under a volunteer co-ordinator who can organise them into an effective work force over the time needed. For major venues use professional organisers and promoters.

After it is all over do not forget to thank the stars and everyone who has helped you in any way at all, as well as all the volunteers and staff. You will need them again next year, and they will love to help again if they have received recognition for their effort.

Keys to success

Your key to maximising revenue is to remember that the artist will only attract their usual audience, who will only pay the usual fee for that venue. Nobody will go just to support your charity.

The key to making events work is to run them year after year. You will find that there is a steep experience curve, and the second and third time you hold the same event (or one very similar) it will be much easier, cheaper and more profitable. Your helpers become professional, the audience returns (it was such fun the last time) and you know exactly what to do.

Art auctions

There are innumerable events that can be held to raise funds, but art auctions are a particular favourite of mine. At their best they bring out a huge spirit of generosity on the part of the artists, auction houses and bidders, and they are great fun.

Quite extraordinary sums can be paid when several people decide they must have a certain painting. Your expectations should, however, be realistic. The art market varies greatly from year to year and prices follow suit. Not every painting by a famous artist is worth a lot of money. In fact, most works will go for quite modest amounts. Let the auctioneer know that bidding will be a little slower than usual and talk through with him how to handle events if you have reserve prices that are repeatedly not being reached. Celebrities' paintings do not sell in art auctions unless the celebrity has a second career as a well-known artist. Celebrity memorabilia is a different event entirely.

It is a good idea to move from fine art one year, to water colours the next, perhaps to cartoons the third year and then to sculpture, before coming back to fine art.

Fig. 6d *Don't stint on the quality of your art auction material. Let it reflect the quality of your art.*

Do not confuse the issue by mixing an art auction with an art exhibition. Auctions make money quickly. Exhibitions take up huge amounts of time, and cost money to prepare and ship from town to town or country to country.

You will need to plan your art auction a year in advance, taking time to cultivate all those whose help you will need and to have the opportunity to overcome the setbacks and problems that will, no doubt, occur.

The three elements that need to be brought together are the auction house, art gallery(s) and artists. It is essential to find a sympathetic auction house and art gallery. Never use an amateur auctioneer: the auction must be conducted professionally. If you have one major work of art for a local auction, consider entering it instead into a city auction where it may obtain a better price, and where your local buyer may well send it the week after.

If your organisation is a major national charity or equivalent, start with the auction house, (possibly one of the top three: Sothebys, Christies or Bonhams), looking for a possible date twelve months or so in advance. As you get nearer the date, seek their advice regarding the quality and nature of the works you have collected and the most appropriate way of selling them. Let the auction house guide you on price, order of sale, number of suitable lots, etc.

The artworks

It is much better to aim for thirty or forty pieces of good quality art than a hundred mediocre works. Of those thirty or forty, there will probably be only half a dozen which are outstanding and it is those which the serious buyers will come for. They will not come to sit through the sale of a large number of paintings they are not really interested in. You do not have to sell everything.

Make sure you have somewhere safe to store the works of art and that you are adequately insured. Always use a suitable van to transport the works and check the size before collecting or you could be in for a surprise.

The gifts of artworks will come through because of a combination of the profile of your organisation, the strength of your cause and the importance and connections of the person making the ask for you. As is usual in fundraising, the personal ask from a close colleague is the strongest possible way to attract a donation. Learn the connections in the art world that the great and the good associated with your organisation may have. It is well worthwhile to spend time on this first. Often the best way is to put together a committee of these people. Working together to secure the best quality art will enhance the result and be less work for you, as you will have one committee to organise, rather than dealing with each individual separately. As with all such committees the chairperson is the key and they must be well respected, effective and stay active throughout the project.

The galleries

It is at this stage that art galleries will prove invaluable. Their owners have many connections and an extensive understanding of the art world, of the sort you need. Your committee people should know gallery owners and it is usual to attract at least one gallery to work with you, helping to make the auction a success. Without a committee, you, or others in your organisation, must have such a connection or you will need to seek help from artists known to you. Another route is to talk to the gallery that handles the work of the artist who donates the finest work. In any case, you will need to work your way through all the galleries who handle your artists and interest them in publicising your auction to their customer list.

The artists

But before thinking about the buyers, you will need to reach the artists. Always start at the top, going for the best artists in their field. Once you have one or more major artists, it is much easier to ask others to join them. Take advice about the best method of approach, which is often to have another artist make the request personally. If a major artist does donate, find out if they would be willing to approach fellow artists - that is how major charity rock concerts are put together. A good existing work will sell much better than something specially created. That is fine for merchandising products, but rarely for works of art. Artists may delight in depicting the suffering you are trying to alleviate but buyers may be less enthusiastic about having this hung on their sitting room wall.

Store the works of art with great care before and after the auction. If they are very valuable, use professional storerooms. You will have some left over that can be sold through other outlets or saved for the next time. Always make sure they are insured and move them cautiously. Check the size of the artwork before collecting it. If they are paintings, they will usually be unframed and you will need to frame them for the sale. This can be prohibitively expensive but framers will often do this for free in return for appropriate publicity. It is worth spending a lot of time cutting down on costs by befriending framers. A volunteer with a good voice will be needed to ring round countless companies obtaining all you need, from frames to food, free, to keep costs down to a minimum. (Free drink is essential, food is inessential, and possibly a distraction.)

Once the venue is arranged and the works of art collected, or suitable arrangements made, you will need to create a catalogue for the sale. This is often the most expensive part of the operation. Good quality colour reproduction is essential if buyers are to be attracted to your event. Make sure the works are fully described, their title, size and medium are important. Always use a professional photographer who has photographed works of art before, (do check their portfolio). It is a professional task, especially if they are large and covered by glass. You can recover some of your costs by selling advertising space in the catalogue to your suppliers and others. Set the date of cataloguing carefully, because you will need adequate time to have it printed and to reach the buyers before the sale. That means the setting of a date by which all works of art are ready. Leaflets and advertising are the next highest expenses.

The buyers

Buyers are found through three principal sources. Firstly, through the galleries which already sell works of art by your artists. Secondly, through the great and good in your organisation, including your top donors. Thirdly, through appropriate advertising: try art journals, obtain lists of buyers from other organisations, and talk to journalists about an article on charity art auction bargains. Invite the gallery owner and anyone influential to the private view. (Although your members should know the auction is taking place they should be discouraged from turning up unless they are prepared to bid.)

The auction house will have a lot of advice about the private view and catering on the night. Use the private view as a 'thank-you' to top donors and others - do not forget gallery owners, framers and businesses that have advertised in the catalogue. You should try to ensure the best artists attend and that there is good quality wine as well as soft drinks. As much of the drink, food, flowers, etc., as possible should come free from businesses, for both the private view and the auction itself. (When you have exhausted already friendly companies, you can work your way through Yellow Pages.)

This is a prestige event, so it can also be used for fundraising purposes such as a high price raffle - 'put your business card in the hat.' Have photographs taken for your own internal publicity and to highlight the auction in your external publicity afterwards. Do make sure that there are enough volunteers present to cater for all the guests and make sure no one is feeling lost.

To invite people to all such events you should use quality invitation cards with gold edges and round corners. Select your most prestigious and appropriate person to make the invitation.

The auction proper will take on a momentum of its own and you will need to free yourself from other duties, in order to concentrate on managing the dozens of unanticipated things that occur. Naturally, you will not handle them yourself, but you will need to feel on top of the proceedings by knowing you have allocated all the important tasks to people you can trust and monitoring that they are actually taking place on schedule. On the night, give yourself the freedom to deal with problems by not taking any major task but let yourself float and liaise with key people.

Take advice from the auction house about the date and timing of the event. It is fine for it to be a weekday and early enough in the evening for business people to attend on their way home. Give the audience time to enjoy their free drinks and look through the catalogue before starting. If you have a lot of lesser works to sell, you could hold a silent auction at the same time whereby people write their bid on a piece of paper below the painting and other bidders add their names and bid more if they wish. This can be quite entertaining but do not let it distract from the main event, perhaps by using a separate room.

Try to avoid reserve prices and percentages going to the artists - you want it all! Some artists, however, like to keep their prices up and in difficult times are loath to give away anything when they could earn from it.

The auction house will handle the taking of cheques, etc., at the end of the event and the dispatch of the works of art, but agree on all this beforehand! You will need to dispose of those left over. This can sometimes be done by arrangement with people who bid under the reserve, or those who missed their chance to bid by hesitating. Do not incur storage charges by hanging onto works that are not valuable. Return them to the artists with thanks. If, for some reason, very valuable works are left, auction them off in a regular auction later, but let the artists know this may happen.

   As always, thank everyone personally and make sure you have included all those who helped, regardless of the size of their contribution

On the day

• Let a key person or celebrity speak before the auction to remind everyone to be generous; and, at the end, to thank them (and be prepared to jump up in the middle and enthuse them if things are not going well).

• After the event thank everyone promptly, as usual. The event has not finished until everyone has been thanked, including all the volunteers.

Key to success

The key to successful art auctions is to put as much effort into attracting real buyers as into attracting major painters. Artists will wish to see their work sold properly, for good prices, remember: they have a market in their work to maintain.

Local group fundraising

Your local groups may provide your organisation with a large tranche of its income, but many organisations have set up local groups' networks with no culture of fundraising. Often local groups are started by individuals concerned to take part in the campaigning work of an organisation. They are serviced by a groups officer located in the campaigns department and much of their income raising potential may be lost.

Starting a tradition of fundraising

To remedy a situation like this is not easy. It requires a change of culture, which takes time. I have noticed that traditions often take only two years to become established, so if your groups can be persuaded to undertake fundraising activities for two years running, the third year will largely take care of itself. Having said that, the work of starting the tradition remains. One idea is the fundraising week, outlined below; another is to establish a fundraising contact in each group so that you can work directly with a keen individual. The fundraising newsletter, also mentioned below, can be a strong agent of cultural change. Do ensure, however, that the rest of your organisation is supporting this development and is kept informed of your plans and progress.

Fundraising weeks

One idea is to hold a fundraising week. This allows you to concentrate on your groups for a short period and, by publicising those groups who are keen to fundraise, begin to influence the others. Fundraising weeks are a well-known phenomenon and many of your local group members will also be members of other organisations which have such weeks. The idea also allows you to use national publicity to assist the groups in their fundraising and, of course, most groups will then receive enquiries which may serve to activate them.

You could start with one idea like a sponsored walk, flag day or book sale and ask each local group to carry it out at the same time. That way you can provide helpful materials such as flag day instructions, tins, forms, sashes, T-shirts, etc.

- Let your groups know well in advance what is going to happen. As groups often meet monthly your advance warning should probably go out six months beforehand, with more detailed ideas four months ahead, and any materials for them to use at least three months in advance, (so that the group secretary can distribute them at the next meeting, and catch those who did not attend at the following one).

- It helps to give groups a clear idea of what they can do, and how to organise fundraising events. A groups' guide is useful, particularly if groups have to pay a fee to head office each year and are largely left to their own devices as to how they will raise this money. Your guide should contain very clear step by step instructions on all the basic local group fundraising techniques, including flag days, door-to-door collections, coffee mornings, jumble sales, car boot sales, running stalls, etc. Give your local groups an advice hotline to someone in the fundraising department.

- It is very useful to establish a fundraising person in each group to work with, rather than the group secretary, (who is often very hard pushed to deal with everything else the organisation asks). Offer the fundraiser a few inducements, such as a training day, priority for much reduced goods from the merchandise catalogue, and a chance to meet with other local group fundraisers each year.

- A newsletter really helps as well, especially if it disseminates good ideas from group to group. Groups learn much faster from each other than they will from someone from head office. Knowing that one group has undertaken a certain kind of event successfully can be a powerful incentive for another group to try it, and perhaps to show that it can do better.

Flag days

Flag days are a traditional form of fundraising that everyone is familiar with, as they play a part in the lives of most of our high streets. In some, hardly a week goes by without a charity collection.

Success here comes from the number of people you have out on the streets. Although it is largely a numbers game, the nature of your cause and public profile is important - as is the material you provide, and training for collectors.

- You will need local authority permission to collect. Apply to the Clerk to the Council, and make sure you have permission for all locations in which you wish to collect. Before the event all such permission should have been sought by you, or the direct organiser, and the best collectors allocated to the busiest places. In London and the Metropolitan Boroughs you may still need police permission until Part III of the Charities Act 1992 is brought fully into force. The current timetable for this is: in December 1997 it comes into force for advance applications, and in June 1998 it comes fully into force when the 1916/1939 provisions are repealed. How it is enforced will be affected by the results of the consultation process.

- Collectors need to be organised around officials who give out the cans, allocate collecting places, and, at the end, collect the money and thank everyone.

- Collectors should be 18 or over and must carry an ID card.

- The official organising collectors should give out sealed and numbered tins, making sure that they all come back with the seal unbroken and that they are counted with two witnesses present.

- Collectors can call out and make a noise, so long as they do this without causing a nuisance. Rattling the can and calling the charity name is the customary practice. If the collector is quiet and retiring, people will just pass by. High streets, stations and anywhere there are large numbers of people are the best places.

- Collectors must not stand closer than 30 feet apart, and definitely not together.

- It helps to have
  - sashes for people to wear, clearly showing the name of your charity
  - collecting tins and leaflets to give out to those interested
  - stickers for contributors to wear so that they will not be asked again, and to show their support.

- Keep a record of the amounts that each individual collects and tell them how much it is when you thank them. Collectors will ask who has raised the most, so keep this in mind. They need to ask permission to collect on private property, shop frontage and railway or underground stations.

- Check the Charities Act 1992 on the regulation of 'public charitable collections', including street collections, as it comes into force and make sure you are doing everything correctly. You can obtain copies of the Act from HMSO, St Crispins, Duke Street, Norwich, NR3 1PD, Tel: 01603 622211, or from the HMSO Bookshop, 41 High Holborn, London, WC1V 6HB. Note that this act is being brought into force in stages in consultation with the ICFM and other voluntary sector representatives.

Door-to-door collections

Door-to-door collections are another standby of local groups. Many organisations and societies began with the weekly collection of small amounts of money door-to-door.

Door-to-door collections depend for success, like street collections, on the power of numbers: on how many people are prepared to drop envelopes through the letter-boxes of houses in streets near them and pick them up, bulging with cash, a few days later.

Also, like street collections, they are regulated by the new Charities Act, which should be carefully perused.

Unlike street collections, however, door-to-door collections have a private feel to them. It is often how well-known the collector is that makes the difference, so collecting locally in your own street can be both profitable and sociable. Collectors can call round together, and much of the fear of going door-to-door is taken away by encouraging volunteers to work in their own neighbourhoods with a friend.

The officials organising the collectors need full instructions on how to run the operation and how to account for the money raised.

Door-to-door collections do require materials to be centrally produced. It is well worthwhile looking at several other organisations' envelopes to see which are the most effective and to test out different ideas. How large should the envelope be? What colour? Should you recruit members as well? Do you indicate an amount? All these questions can be answered by testing.

Telemarketing and door-to-door collections

Recently, telemarketing has begun to greatly increase the income from door-to-door collections. A phone call enables you to talk with your national supporters, (who are probably not local group members), about taking part in the collection. It is surprising how many take part, and the results they achieve. If they do not wish to help in that way they may well be happy to sell raffle tickets or take a small cardboard collecting box which they return when it is full. These secondary actions help to overcome the fact that phone calls by an agency are not cheap. Most of the people called will be pleased to help you and to take part in future years, sometimes increasing your local group support.

Training local groups

Training for local groups can be surprisingly effective if you bring together several groups at a time. There is a wealth of experience in local groups, and they will learn far more rapidly from each other than from you or from an outside expert - though it does help to have that outside professional view if their questions can be answered in a frank and knowledgeable way, accepting the limitations of local groups, but showing how these are best overcome.

Government and European Community funds

Both the UK Government and the European Community act like very sophisticated trusts. They have very clear guidelines showing exactly what they would like to support. They also have thorough application forms and staff to assist in the process.

Both the Government and the EU are typical bureaucracies in that their departments occasionally discover they have sums of money left at the end of their financial year which must be spent quickly, or the department's budget will be cut for the following year. So applying towards the end of the calendar year to the EU, or early in the year to the Government, is not a bad idea at all.

It is well worthwhile spending time talking through your application with the relevant official, who can be very helpful. In the case of the EU, you will need to know what is meant by many of the terms in the application forms. These do not necessarily mean what they appear to, and your request will not be considered unless the form has been correctly filled out. You are well advised to seek expert advice from a consultant specialising in EU applications and to talk to people who have been successful in their own applications.

Grants from the UK Government

The sources of Government funds are covered in detail by Anne-Marie Dalton's book *The Central Government's Grants Guide*, published by the Directory of Social Change.

Unlike the EU, funding from both the central Government and local authorities in the UK has begun to shift towards contractual arrangements to pay for services provided by voluntary organisations to those authorities. The outcomes of these services are monitored and evaluated quite thoroughly, as are, increasingly, the more traditional grants. The tenor is for all payments to further Departmental policy and accountability rather than any emphasis the voluntary organisation may care place on that part of their work.

To maximise your income, think carefully (if not laterally) through both the range of Government Departments that may possibly fund your organisation and the range of grants and contracts that may be available within any one Ministry or Department. For example, the Ministry of Defence is a strong funder of the Pre-School Playgroups Association and The Scottish Office has funded Alzheimer's Scotland under their Mental Illness Specific Grant, and Childline Scotland under their Section 10 grants.

European Community funds

In fact, only a small part of the huge sums available from the EU are really for charities, but the trouble taken to obtain a grant can be more than compensated for by the scale of funds that are then available.

Commissioners in the EU are surprisingly willing to meet applicants personally, (particularly from pan-European organisations), and to discuss their applications. The better they know you, (or rather, your organisation), the better your chances of success.

The Commission has offices in the UK and these are a useful starting point for information, though you will send your application to Brussels to be considered.

The EU has large sums of money to disperse but over only a very limited number of issues. Raising these funds is time consuming and complex but there are several sources of help along the way and there can be huge rewards for the persistent.

The Commission of the European Communities

The NCVO publishes a useful book called, *Grants from Europe* by Ann Davidson, which will give you good background information and which offers much more detail than the following brief account.

The Commission of the European Communities maintains offices in each member country. In London the address is 8 Storey's Gate, London, SW1P 3AT. Tel: 0171 973 1992, Fax: 0171 973 1900. This office has a useful library. There are also offices in Cardiff, Edinburgh and Belfast. The Commission itself is at Rue de la Loi 200, 1049 Brussels, Belgium, Tel: + 32 2 299 1111. Officials speak English and are usually very helpful.

The Commission consists of seventeen Commissioners, officially appointed by the Council of Ministers. Their Secretary General co-ordinates the twenty-three Directors General who run the different departments of the Commission. These are known by their numbers, e.g., DG IX, DG XV. You will find that acronyms are popular in the EU as they avoid having to translate titles of organisations, etc.

Each DG that you may apply to will have its own application form. These are long, complex, and not easily understood. Words are used with certain meanings which are not always obvious, but the process of talking to officials, taking advice from other fundraisers who have made successful applications and, where appropriate, talking with officials in the UK or with the NCVO, (which has staff working on the European Social Fund - by far the largest pot of money!) will ensure you do not lose out because of misunderstandings over jargon. When requesting your application form do not also ask about policy matters. Whilst junior officials can send out application forms, only certain officials can make policy statements so your enquiry may be delayed whilst the statement is prepared and authorised. It is advisable to wait about three weeks before phoning to check on progress - don't forget the time difference or the long lunch breaks! Ask your MEP to help if you have any problems. They have good access and are usually dealt with efficiently by the bureaucracy.

Applications are often considered early in the year, (the financial year runs January to December), so it is best to apply in the last quarter of the year before. Of course, budgets are not always fully allocated and funds may become available at odd times during the year so even if you are officially too late with your application it is worth enquiring about the state of the fund. Grants are, usually, only made once in a year and may take months to come through. The programmes the grants are supporting change every three years on average, and so the grants will not be made for very long-term projects (make sure your future funding is secured elsewhere), and you need to be up to date with existing requirements. The EU often requests matching funding which may come from your own government. Sometimes there is a useful fixed percentage for overheads but do not forget to fund as much as is legitimately possible out of the programme budget.

Surprisingly, a lot of successful applications are from relatively small organisations that have decided to put in the effort needed, whereas many larger organisations do not feel they have the time necessary. Indeed, the success rate for organisations that stay the course is quite high. Naturally, your application needs to be correctly made out, meeting closely the requirements of the DG you are applying to for it to stand any chance. Of course, larger organisations do employ staff specifically to work with the Commission.

In the long term, as usual, it pays to build a relationship. Getting to know your MEP, sitting on advisory committees and networking all help on many levels. The NCVO have a helpful book on the subject called Networking in Europe.

Remember that the EU basically deals with pan-European problems and organisations. Your organisation, networks and applications are all strengthened in the eyes of the EU by being cross-border. For example, if your patrons are recognised across Europe this will help applications by adding appropriate integrity. The EU also appreciates demonstrable government support for your organisation.

Another approach is to undertake work directly for the Commission. Check the Official Journal for all contracts put out to tender; though these do tend to be large scale projects. It also very much helps if your organisation is well known to officials.

The Directors General

The Directors' General areas of responsibility are:

DG I   External Relations, Mediterranean Policy, Relations with Latin America, North-South Relations (includes work combating drug abuse in developing countries)

DG II   Economic and Financial Affairs

DG III   Internal Market and Industrial Affairs

DG IV   Competition

DG V   Employment, Industrial Relations and Social Affairs (includes the European Social Fund, Health & Safety at Work, AIDS, Cancer, Drug Abuse)

DG VI	Agriculture (includes rural development; also free food for distribution to needy people)
DG VII	Transport
DG VIII	Development in Developing Countries
DG IX	Personnel and Administration
DG X	Audio-visual Media, Information, Communication and Culture (includes Citizen's Europe)
DG XI	Environment, Nuclear Safety and Civil Protection
DG XII	Science, Research and Development (includes biotechnology)
DG XIII	Telecommunications, Information Technology and Innovation
DG XIV	Fisheries
DG XV	Financial Institutions and Company Law
DG XVI	Regional Policies
DG XVII	Energy
DG XVIII	Credit and Investments
DG XIX	Budgets
DG XX	Financial Control
DG XXI	Customs Union and Indirect Taxation
DG XXII	Enterprise Policy, Commerce, Tourism and Social Economy (includes co-operatives and some work with non-governmental organisations)

The key funding areas

Among the Directors General the key funding areas are:

Unemployment

The European Social Fund (ESF) and the European Regional Development Fund (ERDF) deal with this area of concern. You should seek advice from the NCVO, and the Department of Employment about the former, ESF Section, 236 Gray's Inn Road, London WC1X 8HL Tel: 0171-211 4732 and from the Department of Trade and Industry, Investment and Development Division, 232 Kingsgate House, 66-74 Victoria Street, London SW1E 6SW Tel: 0171-636 2556 about the latter.

The NCVO currently acts as the clearing house for some £22 million of the social fund. The ESF deals largely with vocational training matters. Here some 50% of the funds go to Government work with the unemployed. It is usual for funds to be given conditional on matching funds from public money.

The ERDF funds go to Community initiatives like RETEX to help areas dependent on the clothing and textile industry, RESIDER for declining steel areas and RENAVAL for declining shipbuilding areas. There are also regional operational programmes started by the national government, and several other categories of lesser importance.

Poverty, families and elderly people

Advice on the current programme can be sought from Directorate-General V, Employment and Social Affairs. The Department of Social Security link is Room 921, Adelphi, 1-11 John Adam Street, London WC2N 6HT Tel: 0171-962 8411.

Women

Advice can be sought from DG X Women's Information Service, Information, Communication and Culture, Rue de la Loi 200, 1049 Brussels, Tel: + 322 299 1111.

There are grants for training for women and projects and studies to promote equal opportunities. Grants are available for women setting up in business, with innovation and areas of high priority having been important criteria. There have been grants for projects to encourage equal treatment for girls in education and vocational training. There is also a Women of Europe Award for a woman, or a group of women, making an outstanding contribution to EU integration. Funds are available to ensure gender issues are addressed in overseas development.

People from ethnic minority groups

In the past, ethnic minorities have not been funded specifically. There are funds that can be tapped, however, under other headings. DG V, for example, has a small budget that can be used to help migrants. Migrant children can be a special category and the ESF has been used for the education of migrant workers. Grants are there to improve the supply of housing for migrant workers and their families.

People with disabilities

Information can be obtained from HELIOS office at DG V, C4 Avenue de Cortenburg, 1040 Brussels, Tel: +32 2 735 1671. The HELIOS II programme which ends in December 1996 covers a wide range of disability related activities. It includes part of HANDYNET a computerised system information system on disability questions. There are various other areas of disability that can come under the Commission's remit including the education of children with special needs, the promotion of research and development of new technologies and transport information for travellers with disabilities, etc.

Human rights

For information on grants for humanitarian actions and the defence of human rights, contact the Commission's Brussels Office. These grants have been quite substantial, with over £3M allocated for work by NGOs, with priority given for direct aid activities in the EU and in third countries.

There are also grants for NGOs working on human rights education and with humanitarian aims, etc. Much of this goes through the Human Rights

Foundation to projects with a practical direct impact, though research and seminars are considered. The address is Human Rights Foundation, 13 Rue Van Campenhout, 1040 Brussels. Tel: + 32 2 299 3243.

DG VIII has had £13M to support human rights and democracy in developing countries but Latin America is covered by another budget in DG I.

Education and culture

The Community provides funding for inter-EU co-operation, exchanges and mobility grants. For guidance on funding try Management Services and Public Relations Department, Central Bureau for Educational Visits and Exchanges, Seymour Mews House, Seymour Mews, London W1H 9PE. Tel: 0171-486 5101 or the British Council, Central Information Point, 10 Spring Gardens, London SW1A 2BN. Tel: 0171-839 4382.

Funding is also provided for such cultural activities as exchanges, the restoration of historic monuments and conserving and promoting architectural heritage. Also possible is funding for training and mobility scholarships in art restoration.

For information on funds for sport try DG X, Audio Visual, Information, Communication and Culture at the Commission's Brussels address, Tel: + 32 2 299 9366.

Outside the EU

NGOs with aid projects of various types and education projects for the EU countries are well served by DG VIII. There is also a UK representative on the NGO Liaison Committee EU-NGO Network, c/o CAFOD, 2 Romero Close, Stockwell Road, London SW9 9TY, Tel: 0171-733 7900.

Two useful documents are *General Conditions for the Co-financing of Projects Undertaken in Developing Countries by Non-governmental Organisations* and *General Conditions for the Co-financing of Projects to Raise Public Awareness of Development Issues, Carried Out by Non-Governmental Organisations in the European Community.*

Eastern Europe is well served by the PHARE programme which also has a fast track programme called BISTRO which can make grants under £50,000 and can reply to completed forms in six weeks.

The environment

For the environment, civil protection and nuclear safety try DG XI, and for Energy try DG XVII. In the UK contact Environmental Protection, Central Division, Room A132, Department of the Environment, Romney House, 43 Marsham Street SW1P 3AT, Tel: 0171-276 8146. At the European level try Secretary General, European Environmental Bureau, Rue de la Victoire, 1060 Brussels, Tel: + 32 2 539 0037.

The fifth environmental action plan runs from 1993 to the year 2000 and concentrates on preventative measures, e.g., rational use of resources, decrease in production, the efficient use of products and their re-use and recycling, energy efficiency and waste management.

The amount of funds available is relatively small by EU standards. The ESF, CAP and RDF all play a part in funding. The EU financial instrument for the environment (LIFE) has funds for actions related to the fifth environmental action plan. Check details with the Department of the Environment (address above).

There are also a small number of funds with the King Baudouin Foundation at 21 Brederostraat, 1000 Brussels, Tel: + 32 2 511 1840. These are primarily for Belgium but some seminars and research projects have been funded. Recent concerns are social issues, the environment and land use planning.

There are other sources of funds related to scientific research, awareness, education and training, the coastal environment, animal welfare, rural development, biotechnology, energy saving and work on alternative energy sources.

Health

The relevant departments are DG XII for medical and health research and DG V for public and occupational health.

Research is covered by the Fourth Framework Programme which runs from 1994 to 1998. The six areas for funding are:

i)   Information technology/enabling technologies

ii)   Industrial and material technology

iii)   Environment and lifestyles

iv)   Life sciences and technologies

v)   Energy

vi)   Human capital and mobility (travel by post-grad researchers).

There are also sources of funds related to cancer, AIDS, alcohol abuse, drug abuse, public health, child abuse, road safety, disaster relief.

Consumer interests

The key Department is the Consumer Policy Service at Rue Guimard 10, Brussels, Tel: + 32 2 295 1720. In the UK the equivalent is Consumer Affairs Division, Department of Trade and Industry, 10-18 Victoria Street, London SW1H 0NN, Tel: 0171-215 3280.

The Consumer Policy Service has a relatively small budget but seminars which have been funded through research projects are unlikely to be successful. However, you should check the current priorities with the London Office.

There is also a useful publication called *EU Research Funding* available from the Commission's London Information Office.

Company giving

Companies can help you in many ways and each way requires a different approach. If your charity is non-controversial and obviously a good cause, you stand a chance of receiving company funds. Companies are not, however, major sources of income for most charities and give far below the level of American companies. In the US it is part of the corporate ethic to put money back into the community from which your profits derive, or at least in which your workers live. Community Chest programmes, which do just that, have long been a feature of the American way of life, but have not had great success in the UK.

Companies are, however, a lot more organised and less secretive than they were a few years ago. Business in the Community, the Per Cent Club, the Action Resource Centre and the Association for Business Sponsorship of the Arts, have all played their part. The Directory of Social Change publications have also helped strip away the mysteries about who has given to whom.

Business in the Community aims to ensure that businesses are socially responsible and also practically involved with their local communities. Education and Training, Urban Regeneration, Employee Volunteering, Women's Economic Development, Local Economic Programmes and many others are all excellent examples of the programmes that Business in the Community fosters. Enterprise Agencies are also a feature of its work, providing varied assistance to small businesses to develop. Other partnership programmes include the Action Resource Centre that provides secondments and gifts in kind for community purposes. A good secondment of skilled personnel can be of incalculable benefit to a charity, though the cultural differences take some getting used to on both sides. REACH, the Retired Executive Action Clearing House, can be of similar benefit, though after a lifetime of commuting, their executives often prefer to work outside London. Business in the Community will provide information on all its programmes. It can be found at 227A City Road, London, EC1V 1JV. There are also regional offices.

The Per Cent Club earned its oddly unsatisfactory name because the goal of even one per cent of turnover, or profits, to charity was held to be wildly over-ambitious. However, Club members do publish a great deal of information on their charitable giving, and over 100 major UK companies are members. They are listed in *Guide to Company Giving* by The Directory of Social Change.

Company trusts

Many major companies have set up charitable foundations and they are approached in the same way as trusts. Some have highly developed aims and objectives while others appear to give at random. There is a pattern to the development of these trusts. At first, the trust exists as little more than a bank account for the companies' charitable giving, (often decided by the Chairperson or CEO). Then the trust acquires a committee and a more settled donations policy. Later on, it may acquire its own capital and begin to move away from a donations policy that, in any way, reflects company objectives. These trusts may be named after the company, the original owner, or may just have an insignificant name to put would-be applicants off the scent. One major company is famous for always giving anonymously.

Many companies, (and individuals), use the Charities Aid Foundation (CAF) in preference to setting up their own trust. They give their donations, or covenant a sum, to CAF and then tell CAF how to distribute this money. Alternatively, they use the CAF voucher system to direct money to appropriate charitable causes. The charity receives a CAF Voucher which it cashes in like a cheque with CAF. A small fee is charged for this service, which incidentally goes to the National Council of Voluntary Organisations (NCVO) which created CAF.

The marketing budget

Companies' advertising budgets can also be tapped. This is usually where the money comes from when you ask a company to take an advertisement in your concert programme. The trick here is to imagine how you can help the marketing managers reach their goals. Does the company sell to children, pensioners? Do you have a schools' programme where, with some lateral thinking, the school, your organisation and the company can all benefit? Do you have a large donor-base that matches the characteristics of a company's target audience? What are your members buying anyway, and would they like to see part of the price they pay coming back to their favourite charity? For once, look for solutions to company problems rather than solutions for your problems.

If you have a large membership of professional people a company may be interested in selling those people a range of financial services through advertising in your newsletter, or by paying to mail to your members, (ensure you are registered for trading in the Data Protection Register and your members have agreed to this use of their personal details).

If you have the sort of organisation where people enjoy the outdoors, many companies will want to reach your members to sell them boots, rucksacks, sleeping bags, etc.

If the company is looking to market its product with a new socially responsible image, then they may wish to sponsor activities that will help with this marketing concept. For example, Reebok sponsored a World Tour by internationally known rock stars for Amnesty International, which went to several countries around the world and was a massive sell-out gaining huge publicity, but the cost was equally large and this level of sponsorship is unfortunately very rare.

Some airlines now help good causes by collecting funds via an envelope in the in-flight magazine. This may come from the marketing department or the social responsibility fund, or the charity may be required to pay for the material so that the company only gives its time. Do not be surprised if a company has no budget for that kind of venture and can only provide services which it has already budgeted for. If you do not have a more productive use for that money do not say no on principle.

Beware, however, if companies just want to put your logo on T-shirts or other goods, without any money coming directly to you. Buyers will expect this to happen (which is why they bought the goods), and if your logo is worthwhile using it is worthwhile paying for. The publicity you achieve will be negligible but the income could really help. Once you have given away your logo you will find it hard to sell it to another company.

Sponsorship

You will usually find that most of your money from the companies' marketing budget will be given in the form of sponsorship.

Sponsorship is assumed to be another distinct area and if you are in the arts, music, or sports fields, then you stand more chance than most, (though sponsorship of major sporting events is really just advertising by another name). Much sponsorship is not wholly and exclusively a business expense. Entertainment comes into this category, and the charity may have to produce two invoices to separate out these elements.

You will find *Hollis Sponsorship Yearbook* invaluable in locating sponsors, and keeping up to date with developments. The address is Contact House, Lower Hampton Road, Sunbury-on Thames, Middlesex, TW16 5HG.

Company sponsorship is often planned a year or two in advance, so write early to the person responsible for sponsorship. As far as possible, try to give your potential sponsor a clear idea of the advantage they will gain from sponsoring you. Will this be in reaching clients, gaining prestige, impressing business contacts or rewarding favours? Will it enhance their corporate image, give name awareness, promote a certain product, benefit staff ? How will their name and yours be linked? Exactly what publicity will they obtain and in what form, e.g., posters, signs on stage, TV coverage? Will their name be part of the event name, so that it will always be used in conjunction with that event?

Remember, in a recession sponsorship is often heavily curtailed because its direct benefit to the company is hard to measure and spending which offers perks to company employees or directors is easily cut.

If you are being imaginative in your discussions with companies and suggesting they put up huge prizes, such as £1 million if six dice come up all sixes, or a golfer hits a hole in one, or even suggesting that they sponsor a world rock tour, then it is worthwhile suggesting that they can insure against these events happening or a non-show by the rock star. This means that, effectively, the company pays a premium and removes the risk and liability.

Arts sponsorship is one area where huge sums can be obtained, and is a specialist field in itself. I would recommend *The Arts Funding Guide*, edited by Anne-Marie Doulton, published by the Directory of Social Change.

Charities that engage in serious sponsorship always ensure that they have a written contract, which makes sure each side knows what is expected. A mutual misunderstanding may have been Oscar Wilde's recipe for a perfect marriage but it won't work for a sponsorship deal. Both organisations' objectives have to match; they have to understand the effort and resources they will put into the project and a controversial association cannot be hidden if a contract has to be signed.

In general, charities obtain much less than they imagine possible from businesses. Profits are for investment and shareholders not for charities. Unfortunately, many innovative schemes can waste a huge amount of company time, for very little reward.

The social responsibility fund

Another company budget is that for social responsibility. To tap this budget you need to be able to command a high profile and to be the kind of organisation that the company's customers love to support. Do not feel you are doing the company too many favours. Interestingly, a survey of European youth has shown that for those under 25, it is the major companies' brand names that have the integrity and charisma, though the charity connection does add a competitive edge to a popular brand name. Again, imaginative schemes with a high profile get the best results. Think out how the company can obtain something special for key customers, suppliers or other significant people they do business with. Celebrities are an obvious link.

Cultivate your celebrities carefully, so that they understand how important it is for you if they can act as your ambassadors at company related events. Think beyond a celebrity performing for you for free. All that often happens is that you save their fee for the night and have the headache of putting on an event you know very little about running. Many charities would be better off paying the celebrity, which would allow them to hold the event at the best time of year and actually pack the most appropriate venue, rather than have it two thirds or half full.

Think about secondment of staff to your charity. Could you use a first rate accountant for a year? What would they get out of working for you? Sometimes this arrangement can be mutually beneficial, as companies restructure or individuals need to broaden their horizons and experiences. Often the association persists long after the official period is over. In many cases, however, companies simply wish to be associated with a good cause and to be thought altruistic rather than just profit-oriented. In these cases, your charity will need to have a high profile and be safely non-controversial. It should deal with subjects that the public at large have a great deal of sympathy with, such as medical charities, pets, and children, all in the UK.

The Chairman's fund

Of course, you can go straight for a company donation from the Chairperson or CEO, though it is still best to do your homework and look at the previous pattern of giving. Then you will be presenting the most attractive part of your organisation's work, as far as he or she is concerned. For most smaller companies this is the only route. As always, do not assume knowledge of your charity, and be very specific in stating what the problem is and how the money will be spent to alleviate it. Ask for specific amounts. If successful, ask again the following year, after having reported back on how the money was spent and what it achieved.

Companies want to create goodwill in their locality and a great deal of company giving is done locally. Your local group may have more success than you would from the centre. They also like to be responsive to their workforce. Many company schemes are dependent on ideas that must originate from their workforce.

The dreaded VAT

Take advice about both your VAT situation, and how income tax is levied on donations that are charitable, or part charitable. Both the VAT Inspectors and the Inland Revenue have offices dealing exclusively with charitable giving, and the position is often more complex than the untrained eye would ever suspect.

Employee giving

Check to see if the target company has an employee scheme whereby the firm will match employees' donations pound for pound. Payroll giving was once heralded as the great step forward in charitable giving, and every charity wrote to the top 100 or 1,000 companies suggesting they set up a scheme, and include them in the beneficiaries. Dealing with that horrendous postbag probably caused a major blip in the economy.

Charities seem to have settled on two approaches. One is simply by reminding their supporters that they should enquire at work about payroll giving schemes and try to include their charity in any such scheme. The second is more dynamic, and involves setting up a volunteer team to visit companies and introduce the charity to the workforce.

Both schemes have had mixed receptions. The former is hard to judge. Income from payroll giving may be increasing, but is this due to the fundraising effort, or to an increase in supporters, (or support itself), or to a natural rise as payroll giving spreads around the country? The latter has worked well for some charities and not for others.

Payroll Giving Schemes are set up by companies under the guidelines laid down by the Inland Revenue and published by HMSO. Money raised for charity in this way is given to a Charity Agency that distributes the funds to the

Fig. 6e *After the first year, profits from affinity cards really stack up.*

appropriate charity, taking a small percentage for administration of the scheme. Some Charity Agencies are long standing, and some have been put together by groups of charities pooling their resources. It is rare now for a charity to set up its own agency. The CAF's 'Give As You Earn' scheme is the most commonly used by companies and most major companies are happy with their charity agency arrangements. Charity Agencies do not have a say in how the money is distributed, and therefore do not need to be approached.

Affinity cards

In the heady days of the Eighties, a number of charities made huge sums by teaming up with banks to bring their members a special credit card, from which the charity received £5 for each card taken out and 0.25% or so of the turnover on the card. Charities with a million members were overjoyed when anything from 5% to 10% of their membership took out cards, netting them a windfall of

£500,000 followed by an extraordinary amount several times larger than that, as the 0.25% on the huge sums going through people's accounts began to kick in.

The cards were well designed and well marketed and supporters felt good about spending. Many took out the card just to give the charity £5, (why not?) and then found an additional source of credit very useful. Now, banks are more likely to require that the initial £5 is used to pay for the mailing to your members.

An affinity card also helps to build the synergy of your fundraising, placing your organisation alongside those trusted charities that are seen as full of integrity and clout.

Negotiating with banks

Today we have got used to using a plethora of credit cards on a regular basis, often with a high level of debt. But the banks are a lot more cautious, and it can take a long time to persuade your favourite bank that your supporters are the right sort of people for them to bother with. You may be well advised to try a link with one of the American banks currently entering the market.

If you have over 100,000 members, mostly in income groups A, B, C1, you stand a chance of agreeing an affinity card deal with a major bank. Be prepared to negotiate hard over the terms. If any of the great and the good on your board, or known to you in other ways, have connections at a senior level in a major bank, it is worthwhile seeking an introduction. You are more than likely, however, to find yourself negotiating with a marketing manager who has a small budget to develop credit card sales and who has never given to a charity in his or her life, but retains a vivid mental image of the worst charity shops.

- If you have carried out professional demographic surveys of your support base and had the results analysed by an independent agency, that will certainly help. If you haven't, it's time you did.

- If a bank agrees, before you accept their terms check with other charities for a comparison. Terms vary a lot, including the number of times a 'free' card must be used in a year, and how soon after receiving the monthly statement your supporters need to pay before being charged interest.

- It will be a great help for you to keep up a series of regular meetings with your bank contacts, if only to remind yourself of all the ways in which you should be putting the offer in front of your supporters. If you do this fastidiously, you will be surprised how much money you make year by year.

Designing the card

You will need to design the card. This is the enjoyable bit. After bringing the concept through your committees, winning a good deal from the bank, and the days of meticulously reading the small print on the contracts, you can indulge your creative flair on the design. But remember, the design should make it easy for anyone to take out and use in public. They will not do this if it is ugly or in bad taste. Wildlife and sunsets work very well, victims and sufferers do not, logos are just about OK - you should be able to do something more imaginative.

You will have to have your logo copyrighted if you are seeking a Visa card as they require legal protection in using your mark.

Marketing the card

- Inform your members by separate direct mail. As with appeals, the response will be much better than it would as an insert in your journal, and the additional mailing costs will easily be repaid by the increased take-up.

- Let all your new members know in their new members' pack that you have an affinity card. (New members are at their most appreciative of the organisation, and more willing to help now than they are likely to be again.)

- It is essential that you keep reminding all your members, at frequent intervals, that they can have an affinity card. Whenever you ask for money, mention that it can be paid for by your affinity card, which will mean the gift goes even further.

Key to success

As with legacies, the real secret of success is to remind people constantly of the opportunity. Eventually, they will feel the time is right for them - but that time will never arrive if you rely on their memories of the original invitation. Having your supporters wondering if you still do a card is not conducive to its being taken up. Your supporters undoubtedly belong to several other organisations, and the chances are that they are being reminded by one or more of these about their own affinity card.

Warning

Be aware that banks nowadays are a lot more meticulous than they were in the Eighties about who they give cards to and how high the credit limit is. Your members may not receive anything like the credit limit they had previously, and may not receive a card at all. (Incidentally, the bank is obliged to tell them if this is due to a bad credit rating).

You will receive a number of calls on this subject, but they should be referred to the bank, who will give you a contact to sort such problems out. Do not get involved in approaching the bank on a member's behalf.

You will need to obtain permission to deal in credit, as you will technically be offering the card to your members. This is covered by permission from the Office of Fair Trading and is not the legal minefield it appears to be. Your bank or the Office of Fair Trading will supply you with an information leaflet.

Grant-making trusts and foundations

Your charity may well have begun with a grant from a grant-making trust. Trusts often like to fund innovative projects for a year or so, until they find their feet and generate resources elsewhere. As a rule of thumb, trusts prefer not to become permanent funders though many will entertain an application from a charity which they helped start for a new or crucial stage of its development.

If your organisation is a new charity, this gives it both a great opportunity and a problem, as you have a relatively short time to get off the ground financially. The backing of a major grant-making body can help, as it shows you are considered worthy of their funds, but you will also need to develop your public profile rapidly to attract alternative funding and support from the public.

In the search for publicity you might even find that a grant from a well-known trust is news in itself - but the real story is your work and how it will alleviate a serious problem.

Researching trusts

Your Bible for this is the *Directory of Grant Making Trusts* compiled by the Charities Aid Foundation. The Directory is large and forbidding, but essential reading if you are to research all those trusts who could possibly help you. (It is by no means an exhaustive list of all possible trusts but will keep you busy for quite a time.)

If you require an easier source book or more in-depth knowledge of the larger trusts, a directory of the top 200 trusts is published by the Directory of Social Change. They also publish a companion volume of the top 200 grant-making companies. These directories are updated every year and new entries appear, so it is well worth being on their publications mailing list.

Target your trusts carefully and try to learn as much as possible about them beforehand. The Charity Commissioners hold all the accounts submitted by charitable trusts. You can look at them on the Commission's premises. If you are going to look at several, it helps to phone first with their names.

One revelation is the size of the average grant. Even for large trusts it can be between £25 and £200. The variety of grants given is also a surprise, indicating just how wide objectives can be stretched.

There is a lot of mystique to trusts. They are often ancient bodies set up under the will of a philanthropic forebear for purposes which were noble in their day, but can now strike us as rather quaint. They may have wished to assist the gentlewomen of their parish who have followed a certain branch of a religion but fallen on hard times, ie. , have become 'distressed'. The will may leave the annual proceeds of two fields to this purpose. The fields may now, however, be in the heart of London and earning a huge fortune in rent from amusement arcades.

Only recently have changes in the law given the Charity Commissioners leeway to begin to consider the varying of such wills. In some notable cases this has unlocked huge amounts of money, though there is a real and reasonable reluctance to greatly change what is, in effect, the wish of the deceased, or to guess what their interpretation of the current situation might be if they were still with us.

Using your contacts

Once you have ascertained which trusts, according to their objectives, can give to you, and which of them are most likely to, the next stage is to match up the great and the good on your organisation's governing body with the trustees of the charitable trusts you wish to approach. Let your chairperson write and call round all the people who may be connected in any way with someone who is a trustee of a grant-making body and seek their help either towards a donation or towards a new contact on the right trust.

Writing the application

- Some trusts have application procedures. If these are mentioned in a directory, obtain a copy and follow them.
- Stunts and 'creative' applications do not usually work with trusts. The best tone to adopt in your application letter is one of efficient enthusiasm.
- State your case clearly on the first side of your letter of application.
- Make it clear exactly which problem you are trying to solve, how you are going to do that, why you think you will succeed, and how much you are asking for, to be put to exactly what purpose.
- It helps the trustees to know what you have already done to raise funds. They will prefer it if you have tried other sources first.
- If you have annual reports and accounts they should be enclosed. If not, the audited accounts will do. If you are starting up, a statement of your financial position would be helpful.
- Do avoid professional jargon and do not assume the trustees are familiar with your work. Make sure you give all the relevant facts to build up a complete picture. How many people will you help? When, where, and how long will it take? Why do you need this amount of money? For exactly what, and why should that help rather than something else? How do you plan to replace the grant when it runs out?
- It is rarely possible to explain all about your work in a covering letter, so it is well worthwhile adding any additional literature or leaflets that you have which will support your case. Make sure these really are relevant and add to what you are saying in your letter.
- Do not leave the trust with the impression they will just be asked to fund again next year or see the project close. If you really need money for three years, say so, but explain what will happen to the project then.

Trusts usually have a focus for their objectives, and it will usually be the case that you are asking for funding for a particular, concrete project rather than core funds. This case can be made separately, outside the covering letter, and should be in as much detail as possible without being unreadable.

Do not send the same letter to hundreds of trusts. Most trusts, especially the largest, have a mountain of applications each week, many of which are completely outside their objectives. This only annoys the trust and could damage a later, correctly-made application by giving a poor first impression.

By all means call the trust beforehand to discuss your application, and afterwards to see if it has been shortlisted. But remember that the majority of trusts have no paid staff, so it is only worth calling the very largest that give out their telephone numbers. Most trusts meet infrequently - perhaps every three or six months or sometimes once a year.

Once the trust has received applications and their secretary has sifted them, the trustees, having a large measure of independence, will make up their own minds about whom to support. In doing so they will draw on their own personal knowledge and experience, which is often considerable, take advice from the secretary or 'correspondent', and add any research they feel is necessary. Anyone who can spend time with a trustee and whom the trustee finds reliable can help. Though this is often thought of as the key way to obtain money from trusts, the simple written application will usually be your main tool.

Developing a relationship

You should develop your most likely trusts and those that have actually given to you as you would any other major donor. (Do not forget to thank them and invite them to see how you have spent their money.) You will also be surprised how effective it can be to send them a regular report on the work they have funded.

The National Lottery

Many charities have claimed that the National Lottery has taken funds that used to go to them and that, with only a small proportion of the stake going to charitable causes, there is a net loss of income to the charitable sector. Others have questioned the grant making policies of the Lottery Board. Be that as it may, the Lottery represents a significant source of potential income and one that should not be overlooked. There are five categories within which your application must fall. Each has its own distributing body, criteria, eligible applicants and eligible projects. The five categories are: The Arts, Charities, Heritage, Sports and the Millennium Scheme. Each of these has its own pack, leaflets or application form, and it is advisable to make contact with them before applying, as it is unlikely your application will be considered unless it is accompanied by the correct form. As the Lottery has only recently begun running, some of the details given below may well change in the near future.

The Arts

The distributing body is the Arts Council of England, (Lottery Department, 14 Great Peter Street, London SW1P 3NQ,. Tel: 0171 312 0123) which distributes an application pack and a *Detailed Guidance to Applicants* booklet. The fund covers all art forms and capital projects. The minimum grant given is £5,000 though joint proposals are possible for larger scale shared facilities. Decisions take up to six months.

Charities

The distributing body is the National Lottery Charities Board. The only way to apply is to phone for an Application Pack, (Tel: 0345 919191). You need not be a registered charity to apply but must be a benevolent or philanthropic organisation. The criteria for grants change each year. In 1995 the main criterion was that projects should address the needs of, or create opportunities for, people and communities disadvantaged by poverty. The minimum grant is £500.

Heritage

The distributing body is the National Heritage Memorial Fund, (Heritage Lottery Fund, 10 St James Street, London, SW1A 1EF. Tel 0171 747 2087/6/5/4/3/2). Apply first for their Guidelines and Application Pack. Eligible projects are those which help secure, conserve, improve and enhance public access to, and appreciation of, tangible heritage assets and add tangible benefits to tangible assets. The minimum grant is £10,000. Applications will be considered by the trustees within five months.

Sports

The distributing body is the Sports Council for England. To apply, ring the Lottery line at the Sports Council for an application pack. You will receive Consultation Forms which should be sent to all relevant organisations a few weeks before submitting your application. Eligible bodies are only those dealing with sports recognised by the Sports Council. Some sports must be affiliated to their sports national body. Eligible projects are essentially capital projects. Equipment purchase is not eligible unless part of a capital project, a major item to be used for six years and permanently on site, or a pool of equipment for a single sport or for more than the local area.

The Millennium Commission

The Commission will receive money until 31st December 2000 to provide funding for projects to assist communities in marking the year 2000 and the beginning of the third millennium. Phone 0171 340 2001 for a copy of the *Introduction to the Millennium Commission* leaflet. From this you will obtain a form to order the Proposal Form pack. Application is by competition each year. The

Millennium Bursary Scheme and Millennium Festival Fund will announce their details later. The Landmark Capital Project fund will fund large capital projects. The minimum grant will be £10M. Smaller capital projects of local significance will be funded by sums between £100,000 and £10M.

Agents

Commercial participators

Part II of the Charities Act 1992 created a class of 'commercial participators'. These can be any organisation which is running a promotion for your charity in which it is stated that funds raised will go to your charity. If the organisation is a fundraising business then it is a 'professional fundraiser' which amounts to the same thing and the Act applies in the same way. If the business running the promotion is your trading company then the Act does not apply. There must be a written agreement and in all communications with the public it must be clear how much the commercial participator or professional fundraiser will benefit and how the money will be divided if they are raising funds for more than one organisation. Seek legal advice on the wording to avoid committing an offence.

The ICFM also has suggested wording for such agreements. For example, if you are running a house-to-house campaign, and an organisation is running this for you, collecting covenants but charging you a percentage of the total, then the public must be aware of that arrangement and its financial implications.

Professional fundraisers

These are defined in the Act as agencies who carry on a fundraising business or solicit funds for charities for reward except:

1 Charities, voluntary organisations and connected trading companies and the charities' staff and trustees.

2 Volunteer fundraisers paid less than £5 per day or £500 per year (excluding expenses).

3 Collectors or volunteers who are employed to collect for the charity or voluntary organisation.

4 Radio and TV celebrities making solicitations for charity on radio and TV (but not other forms of solicitation).

Consultants

It can be very useful to take on a fundraising consultant (or hire a fundraising agency) who may have specialist knowledge and experience of, say, capital appeals or computer systems. If you are thinking of doing this you can obtain a list from the ICFM but make sure you talk to several and that you follow up references carefully looking for a good track record. The ICFM advises strongly against payment by results or by commission. This can seem unduly harsh on small charities trying to get off the ground and there are a few fundraisers who will adapt their charges to suit the needs of the charity. For major projects a feasibility study will help you assess whether there is real potential to develop your idea. A fundraising audit can also show up where the gaps are in your fundraising programme. The ICFM and NCVO have a standard form of contract for employing fundraising consultants.

7 Developing and Managing a Fundraising Department

Starting from scratch

If you were starting a new organisation from scratch:

- You would first need to estimate where your likely sources of income lay. Often the initial gifts come from trusts, from the Government or a wealthy individual. In either case, you would need to work out how long this money would last, and estimate the chances of a repeat donation. (Those who have given already are nearly always the most likely sources of additional finance.) If there is a lot still to be gained from the original source, your first appointment might be someone able to further develop this aspect of income, leaving you free to investigate new sources.

- The next step is likely to be the development of the donor-base, and you will need someone to run it who, in the early stages, will also be undertaking the donor development and appeals for extra funds. If you are fortunate and this works well, the position will need to be split to create one position more concerned with database management, and another concerned with marketing.

- After that, it is really a question of following the best-performing sectors; but be careful of building up 'events' ahead of the donor-base, as the latter is a far more stable area of income. Merchandising is often one of the first posts to be created in a fundraising department but, unless the membership/donor-base is at least 20,000, and better still, over 50,000 strong, this may not be financially attractive compared with other posts which move your supporters higher up the fundraising pyramid. 'Following the best performing sectors' should, of course, be reflected in your long-term (three-year?) strategy, which should be agreed with the organisation via the planning process, and properly resourced through the budgetary process. This objective, and the subsequent development of a department to support it, is really at the centre of any successful fundraising strategy.

Ensuring full support from your organisation

It is essential that the whole organisation is behind your work.

- The first step is to nurture your plans carefully through the planning process. The resource implications must be spelled out as early as possible so that further income generation is acknowledged to be based on development of the department. It is immensely difficult to request successfully additional staff members on the basis of workload if this has not been planned and agreed beforehand (preferably a few years beforehand), as you will be arguing for fundraising staff against programme staff, and that is not easy.

- Remember to back up requests on the part of processing departments like Finance and Membership, who will have to cope with the additional income your work produces; otherwise the process will break down, and your financial and numerical reports will be out of date and provide information too late for you to act on. The servicing of your members/donors will also fail and, as well as being less responsive to your appeals, they will leave earlier than they would normally. Members, as distinct from donors, are surprisingly resilient, but it is very unwise to trade on this by letting your service to them deteriorate. They will assume that the efficiency you display towards them reflects the efficiency with which you conduct your programme work.

Organisational structure

The chances are that your fundraising department has grown up on an ad hoc basis like that of most NGOs. Very few are designed from scratch and very few are re-engineered as thoroughly as the pains of most NGO 'restructuring' might suggest.

At the heart of any sizeable fundraising operation is the donor-base. Yet in many organisations this is located in the membership department, whose mission can be to defend the members from the nefarious fundraisers. Often the membership has voting rights and is the political master of the organisation, not simply a donor-base to be nurtured solely for its disposable income. So placing it outside the fundraising department, frustrating though this is, has a logic which may defeat all attempts to relocate it.

This is not to say that you should not put forward cogent arguments for improving the situation, and demand at least a very high level of service both from the Membership department and from the members' newsletter. This is often another key fundraising tool which can be mislocated in any one of several departments (Campaigns, Communications, Membership, the Directorate) and which will cling on, limpet-like, against all encouragement to move it to a new home.

Despite this negative beginning, the fundraising department can gradually become acknowledged within an NGO as a full department in its own right, rather than an adjunct of finance or the ugly duckling of the events programme.

To emerge from these shelters into the light of day, a sense of mission is needed, and with it the clear idea that the fundraising department is responsible for the entire income generation of the organisation, not just for one small corner.

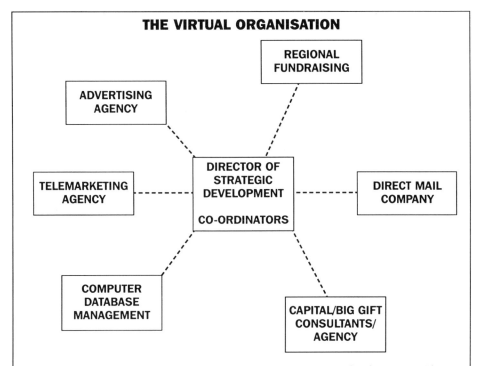

THE VIRTUAL ORGANISATION

The virtual organisation is ideal both for those organisations who do not consider fundraising to be a core competence and in times of rapid change those who do not wish to employ many staff who may lose their positions if growth falters or goes into reverse.

It does demand, however, a very high level of trust and co-operation between the Director of Strategic Development and the key agencies and consultancies involved. These may need to be locked-in to provide exactly the right services at the right time and cost.

There is a strong body of thought that the core competence of many charities and other NGOs is their ability to retain and develop a strong supporter base and that everything else they do can be contracted out or bought in. So be very careful that the links in your virtual organisation provide adequate safeguards and that it is not set up just because the Council wishes to wash its hands of fundraising responsibility.

The decisions to go virtual is a strategic one to meet changing market conditions and most organisations will choose a hybrid using select agencies to complement in-house expertise.

Fig. 7a *The virtual organisation needs few full time staff.*

Possible structures and staffing

There are many ways of arranging a fundraising department and many ways of splitting up the tasks into jobs. The difficulty of setting out a model is compounded by organisations' differing proclivities to use agents or do the work in-house.

- One model is to centralise around the pyramid, using agencies for specialist tasks such as advertising, direct mail, loose-leaf inserts and dispatch of mass mailings, but perhaps retaining the database and cheque processing in-house.

  Here, trawling for new members and donors is undertaken by one member of staff who is responsible for advertising, loose-leaf inserts, direct mail (prospecting) and member-gets-member schemes.

  They should perhaps be responsible for membership renewals as well, (as this is a form of prospecting with a very hot list). This is usually more than one person can do, and so agencies are used to make it all physically possible. This can vary from one overall agency to several (which gives greater expertise, but takes more effort to manage). These can be an advertising agency, a direct mail agency or a space-buying agency, all backed up by various printers and a mailing house or houses.

  To this work is often added that of the direct mail appeals, which sometimes use the same agency as the one used for prospecting. These are, however, quite different disciplines and can be separated without undue loss of synergy. If they are divided then a second staff position may be needed to undertake the work of gaining additional funds from members and donors. This will include, appeals, monthly giving, 'big gift' appeals, capital appeals, legacies and raffles.

  Again, this is more than one person can handle, and agencies can be used. When a major campaign is launched, such as a new monthly giving scheme or capital appeal, new staff may be needed for the duration of the appeal.

- The opposite model, too, is quite appropriate, ie. taking in-house as much work as possible. Once professional staff know enough to instruct agencies successfully, (and they will usually have to instruct advertising agencies very carefully to obtain direct-response, not prestige advertising), they are quite capable of hiring the necessary designers and printers and can cut out the agency commission, and in so doing retain a high level of professionalism and job satisfaction. Cheque processing and database management, on the other hand, are routine tasks that have little 'fit' with most NGOs' culture and can quite easily be undertaken externally.

  In practice, you will find, NGOs seem to oscillate every few years between external databases and internal systems. 'Never again!' is said about each method - until the next time!

- Another possible option is a full service agency that handles all fundraising communications to your donor-base. If this option attracts you, do check the agency's references carefully and ensure that all parts of the agency are as professional as you need, not just, say, their direct mail department.

- Above all, whichever route is chosen, the reporting mechanisms must be first-rate so that feedback on fundraising activity is fast and thorough, allowing adjustments to be made constantly to the various programmes. Advertising, for example, needs daily feedback on response rates to allow press options to be fully exercised.

Departmental officers

A typical department of an organisation of 100,000 members and with £10M turnover could have:

- A Fundraising Director to whom the rest of the department reports: this is a management role involving little or no direct fundraising work. The Fundraising Director should be part of the senior management team and should report to the Director.

- A Trading Officer who handles the catalogue and other merchandising methods.

- An Events Officer who organises national events and liaises with any local groups structure.

- A Membership Development Officer who handles

  - direct mail work (both prospecting for new members and organising internal appeals, including legacies and big gifts), loose-leaf inserts, advertising, and member-gets-member schemes.

  - the Membership Department, processing the income and membership records.

  - the Membership Newsletter. (This gives the organisation the means of developing that warm relationship with members that is essential if you are to maximise your income, though it may not be possible in an established NGO.)

- A Company Officer who works with commercial companies and often Trusts and Foundations as well.

- A Regional Fundraising Officer. This is often the first post that charities establish. A team of local fundraisers across the country reports to the Regional Fundraising Officer in establishing local fundraising drives, setting up local groups and seeking local publicity. The present trend is towards having one fundraising 'Week' in the year, supported by national advertising and concentrating on one or more activities like a door-to-door collection, flag-days or sponsored walks. This centralises the regional fundraisers' functions, but depends very much on the establishment of a network of local supporters.

The officers listed above may need assistants, depending on their workload, and should have an ample supply of volunteers to call upon. This is particularly true of outside events. Volunteers who have helped with these functions in the past are invaluable.

In this kind of set-up you will also need the services of

- an advertising agency
- a direct response company
- possibly a separate mailing company
- an external computer bureau
- the occasional services of consultants as you expand into new areas.

DEPARTMENTAL STRUCTURE

Head of Department

Trust Officer

Membership Officer

THE EARLY YEARS

A typical structure for the early years.
There may be a local groups officer if the organisation has developed that structure.

The database and recruitment materials are often designed and produced in-house.

Fundraising Director

   Trust/Charity Officer
   Legacies

Trading Officer
   Catalogue sales
   Licensing/shops

Regional/Local Groups Officer
   Groups
   Local shops

Events Officer

Membership Development Officer

   Donor-base management
   Advertising
   Direct mail/leaflets

LATER YEARS

This structure can have several external agencies, eg. an advertising agency, a direct mail agency and the database may be held externally.

Officers and the Director may have assistants or specialists working for them.

Fig. 7b *How a typical NGO fundraising department can be structured.*

The charity wing

Many campaigning organisations are legally split between a charitable wing that can receive Gift Aid donations, covenants and all other forms of charitable giving, and a membership-based campaigning wing to which people can belong as members, as well as giving donations. This is the case for organisations like Friends of the Earth, Greenpeace and Amnesty International.

If your organisation has this arrangement, then, as well as the above posts, you may need a charity fundraiser who will solicit gifts from which tax can be reclaimed.

You must be very clear, however, exactly where you want the bulk of your income to go. If most of your work is undertaken by the non-charitable wing, then it cannot receive any money from the charity for non-charitable work, and you may be better off foregoing the reclaiming of tax paid and making sure that most of your income goes to the non-charitable body. The other way round is also quite acceptable and the charity can, of course, legally receive any money the non-charitable body cares to give it. (You will, naturally, want to make sure that donors' wishes are respected.)

One twist to all this is that membership cannot, usually, be covenanted because a covenant is a promise to pay 'for no material consideration', and the usual newsletters and other membership services will amount to material consideration. Covenantors often think they are members, and there is actually no reason why you cannot send your covenantors a newsletter, so long as that has not been promised as an inducement to become a covenantor. You should also be careful not to confuse the covenantors, who may wish to vote as members, or the members, who may think they are members of the charitable trust.

It is quite normal for the charitable trust to grow in size until it is financially the largest partner - legacies are often the cause of this. All things being equal, any professional fundraising campaign will do rather better for a charity than a similar non-charity. People are used to covenants and other forms of charitable giving. Legacies are, in any case, such a huge source of income for most organisations that they often deserve a staff post all to themselves (though this post is often combined with that of one making trust applications).

Staffing for events

A key area for staffing is special events. This is often the area where the fundraising department starts. It is also traditionally an area with a chequered past. Many of the reasons for that are to do with events that have cost the organisation a lot of money at some time or other. The charismatic events organiser who comes to grief over a large-scale production is a familiar figure. Events can, however, be a very valuable source of income and sometimes, more importantly, a great profile-raiser for the work of the organisation.

Events, if they are to be of any size, need a team to run them. This means staff and volunteers. Even if your organisation does not normally use volunteers (why not?) events cry out for lots of dedicated assistance from lots of people. Paying for it all will knock a large hole in your profits.

The number of staff will be determined by the number and scale of events, but there is usually a need for PA assistance, as the work consists both of high-level contacts and negotiations and the more mundane work of endless letters, phone calls, and extensive following up of promises and half-promises before the event, and thorough thanking of everyone after it.

The trading manager role

Often the trading manager's job grows out of the office manager's position, (as does the volunteer manager's job). Running a successful catalogue with 100,000 members, or even 50,000, is a full-time job, though the burden of work does vary through the year. This may be evened out partly by a spring catalogue, but these are not always successful.

The trading manager will, of course, also develop the licensing deals and any merchandising operation to, or with, shops.

Corporate and trust approaches

Your organisation may be one which appeals strongly to the corporate sector. If the potential interest and income warrant it, a full-time corporate officer or even a whole team may be needed. Trusts, on the other hand, rarely require more than one person despite the huge number in existence. Again, this is really a matter for experience.

If either sector responds on such a scale that you have difficulty keeping up with it, then the likely funds will outweigh any increased expenditure in this area. It is very important not to let a flood of enquiries go unanswered as this will give the impression that your work is as unprofessional as your fundraising, and you will lose donations.

The head of department

Naturally, you will need a head of department (HoD) to guide, motivate, monitor, praise and discipline the fundraising staff, and to set targets based on the budget and ensure they are met.

As the work expands the HoD will need to be aware of staff workloads and request assistance or new posts well before there is a crisis. The HoD needs to play a key role in the organisation's long-term strategy development and planning.

The HoD should also be aware that fundraisers are 'role' based whereas most NGOs are 'rule' based, ie. fundraisers see rules as a means to accomplishing the task in hand, and if the rules obstruct this they will bend or seek to overthrow them, whereas the rest of the organisation will probably see rules as guidelines for good conduct in accomplishing tasks properly, and will be less than sympathetic to apparent breaches. In commercial companies the same dichotomy is apparent between marketing and research on the one hand, and the rest of the organisation, particularly accounts and production, on the other.

Job design and staff appointments

It is important for fundraising jobs to have clear boundaries where responsibilities end, so that applicants know exactly what is expected of them. It is also important to set realistic targets, so that staff are not demotivated by apparent failure: an income of £15,000 will be thought a disaster if the budget was £20,000, but a wonderful success if it was £10,000.

Job descriptions are essential in drawing the boundaries around fundraising positions, which otherwise can get very confused. This should be done largely by income source rather than a loose area of work, e.g. 'events' and 'membership recruitment advertising' rather than 'promotions' and 'press work' - in which case who promotes the events in the press? Some organisations have dispensed with job descriptions altogether, as rapidly changing market conditions have demanded flexibility, but that cannot be done effectively without other linked transformations.

As it becomes apparent that a new position is needed, it is essential to

- think through the implications for everyone in the department, as other changes may consequently be required

- look at whether the position is really a permanent one or whether the workload is only a reflection of a temporary increase in income, and whether the work could not better be done outside the organisation or by a key volunteer.

Recruitment

Advertising

You will need to follow your equal opportunities policy in advertising, but within this you might like to consider *The Guardian* on Mondays (media and marketing) or Wednesdays (public appointments), the *ICFM Newsletter*, and *Professional Fundraising* magazine. There are also an increasing number of agencies specialising in fundraising and other 'charity' staff.

Keep your eye on the salaries paid for various fundraising positions. With the huge retreat of state money from welfare provision in the past few years, fundraisers have been in great demand and there is a very limited supply of people with serious fundraising experience, so salaries have increased faster than for most other NGO positions. Some NGO salaries are, however, locked in a time warp so their advertised levels of remuneration will appear derisory.

Make clear in the advertisement:

- exactly what the job entails
- the qualities and experience you are looking for
- the salary and other benefits you are willing to give.

The interview

The interview is far more important than subsequent training, yet most organisations devote much more energy to training.

• Take time to let the interviewee relax and answer all questions fully.

• Make sure you have thought through your questions well and that they will allow you to discover if the interviewee has the experience and qualities you are looking for.

• Make sure that the interviewee talks for at least 80% of the time.

• Talk through their CV with them in detail to see if they have really had the experience it seems to show, or if it is just selective to make it fit the job description and advertisement.

• Think carefully about a written test and 'in-tray' exercise. This can be very revealing.

• Let the staff they will be working with meet the candidates, and preferably have at least one member of the department on the interview panel.

• If, at the end of interviewing the shortlisted candidates, you are not sure which to appoint, do take the time for second interviews. It is surprising how this clarifies issues and how much additional information you can learn.

Interviewees are also interested in how you put the job over to them. It is easy to lose good candidates by making the job seem unattractive. Do not assume, because they have read the advertisement and the job description, that they know all about your organisation or the work they will be doing. How they perceive you as someone to work with is very important. Of course, it will not do to oversell the position. People often remember very clearly what was said to them at the interview. Offers made at the interview, even if only orally, constitute offers under the contract that you are negotiating.

The Institute of Personnel Managers (IPM) issues a very useful recruitment code. Their address is IPM House, Camp Road, Wimbledon, London SW19 4UW.

Induction

Induction to the department is crucial in enabling new members of staff to perform at their best as soon as possible. The objectives of the induction process should be clear and it should be a priority for the HoD to make sure it goes smoothly.

New members of staff will also need to know a broad range of people in the organisation with whom they will be interacting, and how to make the necessary contacts for any research into programme work that they will be writing into their fundraising literature.

Apart from the purely human needs of meeting everyone and getting to know where all the basic resources are, the next most important piece of induction centres on the translation of programme activity into effective fundraising language, whether written, verbal or visual, and on the approvals needed before publication.

Staff development and training

You will find it much more rewarding to think in terms of employee development rather than just training, which tends to mean courses to gain certain skills or improve techniques. These are necessary and important, but assisting staff to develop in a wider context, (perhaps by acquiring new experience, or by moving on in the organisation), or remotivating them after several years of the same type of work, will give your workforce much greater strength and dynamism.

If your organisation is progressive enough, try rotating staff members through different parts of it. It really helps to have worked in departments like finance, communications or campaigns. Staff will not only gain a new understanding; they will also collect friends and allies.

Letting fundraising staff know exactly how the finances of the organisation are progressing will be much appreciated, so long as they can also see where the income they generate and expenditure they incur fits into the overall picture.

Training courses

There are now many well recognised fundraising training courses. The best known are run by the Institute of Charity Fundraising Managers (ICFM) and the Directory of Social Change. These courses provide both basic training for those entering the profession and more advanced training in specialist subjects. The ICFM also runs an annual convention in Birmingham, which is highly recommended. Other courses are advertised from time to time in the fundraising press.

Promotion

In many NGOs there is no career structure as such. People do move from voluntary work to staff posts and then to senior positions, but promotion tends to be possible only by moving to another organisation. Many people are understandably reluctant to do this.

Within a fundraising department this can be ameliorated by training volunteers and staff so that they are ready to apply for vacancies as they fall open. To some extent positions can be shaped for the people moving into them, but this is dangerous if carried too far. What happens if they leave soon afterwards? Can you find another person with the skills that fit this special job? Will you have to restructure the department again?

It is often difficult for staff with special skills like merchandising, trust fundraising, or running events to move to the stage of running a department. More often, the jump is made by those with marketing skills who work with direct mail, advertising, and other direct response media. The transition can only be made by building up your CV to include the skills required, (including management), by training and experience. Sometimes a spell in a parallel position in marketing will help, or a move to a smaller organisation where the 'fundraiser' does everything.

Redundancy

Redundancies are rarely handled well. They usually come in the wake of long financial problems, when the organisation has finally accepted that it should scale down its work and delay has made things so grim that redundancies have to be made with undue speed.

For a fundraising department there is often the early psychological problem of knowing that the net income budgets have not been met, and that therefore the programme will suffer. This is exacerbated when individuals' positions are on the line.

Naturally, as income drops, fundraisers should see their resources increase to cope with the problem. This, unfortunately, does not happen very often, and NGOs are likely to take the foolish step of laying off people equally across departments, or putting everyone on part-time when they should be increasing staff time devoted to fundraising. This only aggravates the situation, and means that fewer funds will be raised, so speeding up any redundancies.

Inter-departmental conflict

Fundraisers are often anxious to complete tasks within strict budget and time requirements. This process is often accompanied by a high level of tension and relative uncertainty about the outcome. It is not surprising that fundraisers can clash with departments working to a different timescale and priorities. For example, another department may prefer to have programme information checked by a particular person, (rather than have an advertisement go out on time), or to meet auditing requirements, (rather than take time to let Fundraising know immediate details of the returns on the day's advertisement).

An organisational culture which respects fundraising is essential in order to create the positive climate that will welcome new initiatives and the resulting changes. An over-dynamic fundraising department which upsets peoples' lives by creating continuous organisational change is rarely appreciated, as most people prefer a quiet, orderly life with a large degree of security. Rapid growth, new employees starting and new programmes beginning mean that staff positions change, and the position of older staff in the organisation changes too. Having been accustomed to being a vital part of a small organisation, in direct contact with the director, staff may feel devalued if they find themselves having to report to a new person in a distant part of the empire.

Preventing clashes and wars saves an enormous amount of time and energy. Once an interdepartmental war has started it can rumble on for years through the evolution of an organisation, weakening it and holding back its development, as well as making the working lives of staff intolerable.

- The key to war prevention and peacekeeping is to anticipate the areas of clash and to agree procedures for staff to follow which meet their needs within the agreed priorities of the organisation. In the customary NGO free-for-all you will find this may not be welcome medicine but it is far better than the disease!

- Thorough planning, which goes hand-in-hand with good communication, helps a lot. If all other departments know that fundraising is going to double the membership in a year they can expect their correspondence to double as well. The post room, Finance and Membership will be able to plan how to cope with the influx, and if the means by which those people will be brought on board is well known, provision can be made for the necessary information to reach Fundraising, and the approval givers can be prepared for the material that comes their way.

- Above all, avoid surprises, so that people can plan to take fundraising needs into account at all levels. It is necessary both to alert senior management, so that they can tell their departments what to expect as part of their work, and to make early contacts among staff at lower levels, so that everyone to be affected is personally informed and brought on board. This also acts as an insurance policy, in case management is inefficient. Above all, don't forget your friends in the postroom!

An organisational culture which respects fundraising is essential to create the positive climate that will welcome new initiatives and the resulting changes.

These transitions need very careful handling with a strong emphasis on understanding just how important the changes are in achieving the organisation's objectives. If this is not clearly comprehended by all staff, change will be vigorously opposed.

How to get fundraising ideas through committees

One of the most frustrating aspects of a fundraiser's life is seeing brilliant fundraising ideas turned down by committees for seemingly irrelevant or illogical reasons. Many fundraising ideas can be agreed by the HoD, but these are usually ideas whose cost can be accommodated under existing budget heads and which do not run counter to any current policy. Other ideas may need the director's approval because they involve interpretation of policy, or have a significant public impact. (Naturally the director must personally approve anything that will bear his/her signature.)

Ideas outside current policy, or in grey areas, or that require additional funds, will most probably need approval by a subcommittee of the council or board which governs the organisation, (this is usually the finance subcommittee on which the head of fundraising should sit). Or they may need approval by the board itself on the recommendation of the subcommittee, or by recommendation from the Fundraising Department to the Director to the Finance Subcommittee to the Executive Committee to the Council - this is not unusual! Any ideas involving something new, like telemarketing, have little chance of success in those circumstances, as it usually only takes one strong individual on a committee to object and the idea will be rejected, or so circumscribed that it is not worth carrying out.

Sometimes, of course, committees just like to say no. They have passed everything for ages and feel the need to establish their authority by saying no to something. If you can sense when this is the case just give in quietly, ask for the ostensible reasons, and bring the project back later with the problems dealt with.

In fact this is often the way forward with complex projects where the committee does not fully understand what is being proposed - they may not even have read the paper, especially if it is long - and needs at least one more chance to discuss the idea. Committees that are pushed often say no.

• Committees respond much better to pulling - having all the positive aspects of the project set out before them. Do not highlight problems but make sure they have been dealt with clearly in your written report. Let committee members raise them if they will, and answer them by understanding the point they are raising but demonstrate that it will be taken care of, or show that, though relevant, it will have minor impact compared with the intended result.

• If you contradict a committee member, do so without signalling your intention by saying 'You may not agree to this', or any such remark that gives them time to frame a negative response. Just make the contradiction directly and clearly. Often this will not meet with a reply at all. (This technique should be used sparingly. It is better to be the friend of a committee.)

• If you can directly answer the first person to speak against the idea, do so. Signs of a fight, before committee members have voiced an opinion, will give them pause to consider both sides.

• Count how the 'vote' will go as soon as you can, and offer a compromise if it helps: 'I think we are mostly agreed on this, but I'll carry it out in September instead, to avoid any problems,' is the sort of remark that lets the chairperson wind up in your favour.

• Cultivate your chairperson, who is usually the key to unlocking committee decisions in your favour. Whatever you do, do not show up the chairperson in public.

• Chat to all the committee members informally in the breaks, but do not use these for obvious lobbying. You are forging relations for the future, not the present, though you can strike a deal if that looks like a good way forward. Work on the committee members before the meeting by keeping them informed of positive progress. Overt lobbying can be very helpful but can also misfire, and you will need to judge this very carefully. Lobbying by local groups really helps if they have elected the council members.

- Large council meetings are often the easiest, because only a few people will speak, and usually only once; you can contradict them emphatically, knowing that their vote does not matter much, but that you will influence the quiet members, who will not vote against something to which all objections have been clearly answered.

- Above all, your confidence in the matter is crucial and means more than the statistics. Self-confidence impresses committees. They feel that they can rely on someone who is self-confident, even if they think the person is probably wrong.

§

Working in a successful fundraising department can be a very rewarding experience, as successes can be clearly recognised. Another satisfying and interesting aspect of fundraising, which lies behind the creativity inherent in the work, is the whole psychology of giving. The next chapter looks at some of the issues involved.

8 Mr and Mrs Chequebook at Home

The psychology of giving

So why do people give away money, and why do they keep on doing it ?

If you cannot answer that question you cannot begin to fundraise, because you will have no real idea of what to say to people that will really convince them to join or donate to your organisation. You may even say many things quite innocently, which will put people off your organisation for life.

Finding out the facts

The simple answer is to ask them. Get together a few groups of, say, six to nine people who have given to your organisation and put a range of questions to them. This is usually a very revealing exercise - but beware. People love to tell you just what they think you want to hear, and it is much more effective if you use a professional agency to undertake these 'focus group' exercises.

Once you have a clear picture of just why people are attracted to your organisation you will need to weigh up the evidence carefully. If they are attracted for the reasons that you set out in your fundraising literature, are they just parroting back what you have said? It is a useful corrective to ask another set of people why they did not join or give to you. It could be for the same reason, and that you are putting people off as well as attracting them.

So you need to test your research against your own professional judgement, but do not just dismiss what people say, if it conflicts with your own views about what is effective. Test out what you learn. If you do not test, you really do not know.

Keeping the relationship alive

If donors have been giving to you for a long time and donating regularly, they expect to see that you have done something positive with their money.

They need not just a thank-you letter, but a way of knowing that their donation has achieved their objective in giving. So reporting back after an appeal, or after the problem you are working on has appeared in the media, makes a big difference to the donor. If they have confidence that their money is well spent, they will give again and again.

Using your newsletter

The usual means of keeping people informed is your newsletter, sent out about four times or so each year. Do you really need to send it out more often? Is three months too long to leave your members in suspense, (or, worse still, leave them open to approach by another charity)? Either way, four issues a year is common and, though the readers will always say that they would give up the newsletter to save you money, they would also rapidly drift to another charity if they ceased to hear from you.

The newsletter also allows the organisation to mature and develop in the eyes of the donor. For example, let them know

- how the needs of the people you serve are changing, so that they will come with you when radical change happens, (as it does every few years in the voluntary sector. If it hasn't happened to your organisation yet, it is unusually unresponsive or about to explode). Prepare your donors for these changes.
- when you take on new staff, and what important work those staff will do
- everything that you find interesting about working for your organisation.
- how much the latest appeals have made, and how you are now dealing with the problems you set out in the appeals. This feedback develops donors' confidence in the organisation, and brings them up the fundraising pyramid, enhancing the warm feeling they have for you - which will develop their generosity.

If things go disastrously wrong, let donors know as soon as possible, and they will give again to help you. If they learn about it from the media, they may feel let down and leave. Always tell the truth in these circumstances and let donors have a clear idea of what went wrong and how you intend to go about putting it right. Do not be afraid of offering donors their money back if you cannot spend it in the way you said you would. In fact, you are obliged to do that. In practice, organisations have found that the gesture is really appreciated, and few people ask for their money back. Often more donations come in. Honesty is a highly valued commodity today.

Varying your communications

As new means of communication develop, be prepared to use them in your fundraising to keep the relationship alive. Nothing kills relationships like repetition.

- Vary the size and style of your newsletter.
- Use video to communicate.

- Do you have an email list of top donors? If so, use it to update them on your programme and to reach them whilst items relating to your organisation break on the news.
- Use the ubiquitous fax machine (but use it sparingly).

Varying the scope, size and style of your communications helps to maintain readership interest, but the content needs to move with the other changes. Keep it lively, but in a style in keeping with your organisation's spirit. You may have a very conservative readership that is frightened of change. (But if that is the case, why is it so? Is your membership profile ageing along with demographic trends, or are you failing to bring new blood into your organisation? Can you shift the trend or should you start new groups of supporters with a different ethos, to secure your income on into the future?)

Motivating your donors

Do not take your donors for granted. Keep asking them what they want out of the relationship - you might be surprised! Surveys, questionnaires, focus groups and telephone calls all serve to let your donors pour out their hearts to you. If you have never undertaken a questionnaire, then you will be surprised just how many people will take great pride in telling you all about their personal feelings for the organisation. This can be immensely rewarding if you have the courage to respond positively to all that you learn.

You may learn that amongst the key motivators are simple rewards that will not take up much of your time and effort compared to their value to the donor. These are likely to vary a great deal from organisation to organisation because the psychology of the donors will be different, but common motivators are visits to your hospital, offices, centre, sanctuary, first nights, etc. Seeing the work taking place is a special privilege for those who have helped to make it happen. Having special access outside the normal visiting hours when no one else is around can be very rewarding for your donor.

Open days

An open day, for example, can really develop the relationship - but you must take care that it does not work against you. Make sure staff are happy to be showing people around, rather than resentful at spending another Saturday at the office. See that the day's agenda is well planned, from travel there and back to refreshments at appropriate times, as well as explaining the work and letting the donors enjoy the experience. Knowing the organisation, they may have lots of detailed questions, and experienced members of staff should be on hand to deal with the enquiries in appropriate depth. Let them rattle old skeletons that may be lurking in the closets, so that they have good answers when their friends ask them similar questions.

Recognition

Certificates and registers of supporters, tree planting in donors' names, and mentions in the annual report are all valuable ways of rewarding donors and building the relationship; but make sure these are ways that your donors will appreciate. That is not easy to do because asking the question directly will often be met by the modest answer, 'Oh no, I would not like that at all,' whereas in private, the donor may well be quietly proud that their name is engraved on the new hospital wall-plaque, or whatever.

Asking donors how they feel other people might respond will often give you a stronger clue to their own likes and desires. Some people could be embarrassed by the kind of recognition mentioned - but they will give, usually anonymously, or tell you their wishes quite clearly.

Personal contact

Often, personal contact is the strongest motivator of all. If you have a director, celebrity or key player in your organisation whom the donors will know quite well, either in relation to your work or from their role in public life, then you have a powerful motivator who can create a lasting impression on your supporters at meetings, and, more effectively, face-to-face. It is likely that this person is very busy, but they will make a strong impact on your major givers or prospective major givers at dinners, or face-to-face meetings at their office or yours.

There are theories to support meetings in either office. I prefer to visit major donors in their own office or home because it is easier to arrange, and the donor is relaxed and inclined to be generous to their guests. At your office you are in charge and have the psychological upper hand but your donor may feel under pressure, which is bad for the kind of long-term relationship that brings rewards to both parties. Under pressure to give, the donor may make a relatively small donation for the sake of form, rather than commitment.

So, if you take the time and trouble to formulate a view on your donors' needs, and test that view in practice, you will gradually learn how to develop the relationship beyond the immediate one-donation-at-a-time scenario to the mutually profitable fields of long-term commitment.

Phoning home

Double-glazing salespeople have given the phone a bad name as a means of communication: but a call from an old friend you thought had forgotten you is a pleasure to receive.

When the old friend is your favourite charity, it is also quite touching and personal. That is not a moment which should be left to chance. Well-planned and thought-out calls are a pleasure to receive. Calls with a cast-iron script are a cause for concern. By all means use the phone to ask for donations of all sorts, but do it sensitively to appropriate people and take great care to ensure that those who have any objection to calls are not phoned again. Make sure all questions asked are eventually answered, though the caller will rarely be able to answer them all and must say if they do not know the answer.

If you have interesting news or information that your members might like to hear, then phone them as you would your friends but, as with your friends, phone those with whom you have reached that stage of the relationship. Phoning someone who has made a small donation to tell them news about a project they will not know of, can be counterproductive, but phoning members to ask them to write to their MP about an issue which has just come up can be very productive. Calling major donors to let them know good news about a project they have heavily invested in will be very welcome. Who calls is important. Anyone who is keen, well-spoken and informed can phone, asking for a letter to be written, but the person who sought the donation from the major donor is the best person to call with the news, unless another caller is obviously of higher standing in the organisation.

Keeping in close touch with your donors can build a lasting relationship beyond the usual telemarketing to lapsed members. The word telemarketing itself inhibits our understanding of the possibilities. To use the phone only to bring back members or reactivate donors is to miss a great part of its value.

Naturally, faxes, email and all other forms of communication are also useful devices for keeping in touch, provided they are used sensitively and imaginatively to build the relationship.

From the cradle to the hereafter

New supporters

Your fundraising will be targeted at your core market by age, education, profession, geographic area, etc. But working exclusively in that market is limiting and you risk the problems many organisations have faced, such as the support base becoming progressively older and older, or that the organisation is seen as representative of only one small part of the population, or only of interest to one segment or gender.

If you devote a relatively small percentage of your budget to testing new ground and investing in new age groups, you will be both opening up the opportunity of discovering that your target market may be much larger than at first envisaged, and also taking advantage of the fact that testing alters the perspective of the market. Seeking new members should also serve to educate all those who are approached and make them more aware of your work. Because such prospecting is in new fields, this may be the first opportunity these people have to learn about your organisation, and therefore, they may in time become supporters.

Conventional wisdom says that people have thought seriously about joining an organisation at least three times before they eventually take the plunge. So it may take, say, a series of advertisements backed by direct mail to eventually open up a new market.

Many organisations have found that their student membership will leave after their student days, but return after marriage and children. Of course, there is no telling if they would have joined anyway, if the student programme did not exist, but it is a common sense deduction to link them together until more rigorous analysis has been done. Sometimes students are an easy catch, but an unprofitable one, and if recruitment is aimed principally at students, who often pay a reduced fee, the membership of the organisation may expand impressively but the income falter. Of course, students make good activists. They have the time to help, but rarely the disposable income, though that will come as they move into the professional classes.

Schools

A few years ago many national NGOs had small teams of educational staff who toured schools, giving talks about the work and concerns of those NGOs. Some of these had great educational value, others were thinly veiled or naked fundraising approaches. Eventually evaluations of their educational performance found most of them wanting in their ability to reach even a small proportion of the nation's pupils or students. To do this thoroughly at classroom level would require huge teams of educationalists.

It is much more likely now to find organisations seeking to influence the national curriculum or teacher training so that their concerns form part of the overall educational process. Naturally, fundraising has been left out of this process though there is good reason to suppose that the impact of environmental studies will keep the green movement afloat for many years to come.

There is still a great deal of money to be made from classroom based fundraising, but it is labour intensive and schools should demand a high educational content linked to any appeal for funds. It helps if your organisation has a strong component of teachers within its membership because they can often be mobilised to support your work and appreciate that you will need to include an element of fundraising.

At a local level, it can be useful to the school for you to run an assembly and to be allowed to ask for funds on the back of that work, but increasingly, schools will be looking for a long-term relationship, which of course will be most effective for you as well. Take the time to talk to teachers and educationalists about adapting your materials and talks for different age groups, and arrange a programme with the school so that you can eventually cover the whole intake. Set out the educational goals you expect to achieve as clearly the fundraising goals, so that the schools can see your objectives. Do check that you are really meeting all your overheads because it is easy for staff to believe strongly in the educational work and fail to realise the fundraising objectives. When you first set up this programme the returns you expect and how you will judge staff performance should be absolutely clear.

Because you are dealing with a great number of individuals, think through various sponsored activities related to your organisation or stay with the simple sponsored walks and sponsored swims, etc. Look at any small objects that children could collect, related to your organisation, that you could then use or sell, e.g., stamps or silver foil (where there is a market). This technique has been perfected by Blue Peter and is a good standby, but do ensure you can cope with the volume of goods you might receive. At a national level you may find it possible to link with a national company that wishes to reach the schools market and is willing to invest a reasonable sum in sponsoring a range of fundraising activities to increase its brand recognition by teachers or pupils.

Don't forget that education and fundraising can also be fun for kids. An element of humour and imagination will go a long way in your schools' fundraising.

Adapting to your market

A full fundraising programme will cover all age groups and all segments of society, adapting to the conditions and psychology of each market as far as it is profitable in the long run. This often requires considerable adaptability on the part of the charity. You may be used to linking celebrities with your advertising in tabloid newspapers, but they will not be effective in the broadsheets. This change of tone and emphasis is often very difficult for a charity's policy makers to accept. It is easy to become used to a certain language, and to fear that another way of writing or putting over the message will not carry the same content, or will trivialise or misrepresent the organisation. You must take care here to make sure that the essential message is clear and be prepared to show how each segment of the population will react to, and understand, what you are saying. It is very instructive to talk to charities already operating in that segment, to learn how their fundraising is received.

§

A key part of adapting to your market is understanding its culture, particularly its moral values. The next chapter tackles some of the questions of morality that may arise during your fundraising.

⑨ Moral Issues

Shock!

The use of 'shock tactics' in fundraising has caused a lot of debate, and in some organisations concern about it has got to such a point that making the simplest case for supporting your organisation may have to be watered down so much, in case someone is offended, that no one will ever feel it is particularly important to help your cause.

Fig. 9a *You can shock but not give offense.*

The distinction between 'shock' and 'offence'

The Advertising Standards Authority makes a very useful distinction between shock and offence. Basically, it is wrong to offend someone; but the nature of many charities' work is such that it is not surprising if it shocks. Shock is a natural reaction to the horrors we are trying to alleviate.

Offence is more difficult to define, but its essence is the gratuitous hurt that people feel when they are the targets of an attack. Unfortunately, this can happen inadvertently if copy is not thought through from the reader's perspective. Naturally, biased and bigoted people will claim to be offended by many things, but anyone intending to put forward a strong case for supporting a needy cause must take that in their stride. Setting out factually what has happened to people, however shocking, cannot legitimately be held to be giving offence.

Individual cases

In seeking to give potential donors the chance to empathise with suffering individuals, it is necessary to let them know just what has happened to those individuals. Group suffering rarely has the same effect, and mass tragedies can only be comprehended through the stories of single people, but you do need to consider the wishes of those people whose plight you depict. Nearly always, they are more than willing for their story to be told, but you should ensure that those who do not wish for publicity are not exposed.

* Changing names and some other details to protect identity is quite legitimate.
* As far as possible, you should identify the people in photographs, which should not be used without thought for the subjects or the reasons why they were taken.

'Composite' cases

The use of 'composite' cases raises more questions. Here charities give a typical example of the kind of person they are setting out to help, rather than giving a true case history. These pictures often combine several case histories into one story. This can give a more correct image of who is being helped by the donor's money, but you should be very careful to make it clear what you are doing, so that people are not misled into thinking you are presenting an actual case.

* A composite should never be a substitute for proper research.
* Be very wary of the copywriting of composites, as this can tend to shift from a typical case towards an extreme, which may not truly reflect your work.
* If in doubt, use real cases, and vary them through your campaign, so that the differences in cases comes across.

Respecting privacy

There are two kinds of privacy that you should be aware of:

- the privacy of the people you are helping
- the privacy of the subjects of your campaigns - members and donors.

The privacy of those you are helping

The importance of considering the privacy of those you are helping is common to both fundraising and issue campaigning. It has been highlighted by cases of disabled people who have felt that they were being made into objects of charity, and not recognised for their talents or for the problems they faced in their everyday lives.

Remember that every campaign carries at least two messages:

- the clear call for funds
- what you are saying in general about the set of people or conditions you are trying to help.

Featuring disabled people in asking for funds can also cast them as helpless individuals. Showing starving children can also carry a message of hopelessness about the country they are in, and depicting rainforest destruction can lead to simplistic assumptions about the perpetrators.

There are no clear guidelines for these cases, but you do need to consider all the messages you are sending, and how they square with your organisation's overall aims and objectives. No one wishes to end up doing more harm than good, and you will often have to make some hard decisions; but that is preferable to inadvertently campaigning against yourself or giving up an excellent fundraising campaign because of uninformed worry. Asking the people you feature for their opinion can be an eye-opener.

The privacy of the donor

When there is a disaster in a small town, everyone rallies round to help. People knock on each other's doors, ring each other up, and write to people further away who could help. This is perfectly normal and praiseworthy human action.

When the disaster is in another country or another town, or even not quite so visible, we are often suddenly afraid that people may be offended if we ask them for assistance, and we worry about putting undue pressure on them to help. This is the fear of poor excuses - and it can paralyse organisations.

Many people feel that they should help, but do not really wish to, and to avoid making a plain statement of this fact, they hide behind a variety of simple subterfuges. First among these is to attack the medium, rather than the message: 'It wasn't that I didn't want to help, but I don't think you should send junk mail, phone people up, spend all that money on advertising or put leaflets in magazines - its such a waste.' If accepted at face value, all this would leave a fundraiser rather baffled in the search for a universally acceptable means of fundraising.

People react differently to different media. Some people love it when their favourite charity calls them up personally. Other people don't like it at all. Some people like to sit and read through long letters explaining what a charity does and why it needs money. Others regard this as junk mail and a threat to trees. There is no universally acceptable means of fundraising, and there will be some objections to everything you do. Be prepared for this, and think through how you will respond to the most likely criticisms.

If people tell you they do not want to receive telephone calls, take note of it and do not call them again. If you cannot record and deal with this you are not ready for telemarketing.

Other media are harder to deal with. When undertaking reciprocal mailings, you should, however, de-duplicate your list both against the other organisation's list and against the Mailing Preference Service (MPS) scheme, and ensure that the lists you buy are similarly treated.

If your targeting is accurate, people may receive several mail shots from you and will see your advertisements and read your loose-leaf inserts. They take this personally, with a touching faith that every communication you send out is targeted deliberately and personally at each individual who reads it. Often you will write to your own members, asking them to join. Even if you de-duplicate (using specialist software to eliminate duplicate names and addresses) bought-in lists against your membership list this is still likely, as people write their names and addresses differently on different forms. Adding a phrase like, 'if you are already a member, please pass this appeal on to a friend' can assist you in not offending your members and increasing your support.

The Data Protection Act

The Data Protection Act, appropriately passed in 1984, sets out to protect personal privacy under threat from the rapid development of computer systems capable of holding and processing vast amounts of information on individuals.

As such, it has failed either to restrict the information held, or to appreciate the benefits of more carefully targeted appeals. The Act merely requires the registration of 'personal data', which is 'automatically processed' (by computer). It does not cover ordinary card index files. The Act does, however, allow 'data subjects' access to that information and to have it corrected or deleted. On making a written request, the data user is obliged to give you a copy of that information. The data user can charge up to £10 per entry for supplying that information. Your request should usually be met within 40 days. If not, you can complain to the Registrar, (an independent officer reporting directly to Parliament) or to the courts.

Most fundraisers will be 'data users', who control the contents and use of personal data on their donors or potential donors. (This can be personal data on individuals as well as companies, charities etc., and includes any information about living, identifiable individuals, even just their name and address.) They must be registered with the Registrar under the various categories for which the data is intended to be used. It is important to register in every category which you are likely to need, as failure to register is an offence. Some of these categories are decidedly quirky, for example, the Registrar regards reciprocal mailings as 'trading' not 'direct mail'.

The Registrar has drawn up a series of Guidelines which can be obtained from the Information Services Department, Office of the Data Protection Registrar, Wycliffe House, Water Lane, Wilmslow, Cheshire SK9 5AF, Tel: 01625 535 777, Fax: 01625 524510, where registration forms can also be obtained. Basic information on the eight Data Protection Principles can be obtained from the Registrar's Internet site at http://www.open.gov.uk and the email address is data@wycliffe.demon.co.uk

When you apply to register you will need to state:

- the personal data held
- the purpose for which it is used
- the sources from which the information may be obtained
- the people to whom the information may be disclosed, i.e. shown or passed on to
- any overseas countries or territories to which the data may be transferred.

Think carefully about every other use of personal data in your organisation and make sure you are registered for it.

You must be clearly aware of, and follow, the broad principles of good practice contained in the Act. These are that personal data must be:

- obtained and processed fairly and lawfully
- held only for the lawful purposes described in the data user's entry
- used only for those purposes and disclosed only to those people described in the register entry
- adequate, relevant and not excessive for the purpose for which it is held
- accurate, and where necessary, kept up-to-date
- held no longer than is necessary for the registered purpose
- accessible to the individual concerned who, where appropriate, has the right to have the information about themselves corrected or erased
- surrounded by proper security.

If, for example, you collect signatures on a petition, the data cannot be used to send those people a request to join your organisation if their details are held on computer, however briefly, unless you are registered for that purpose and the code is followed.

You should be sure that you:

- have obtained the information fairly, e.g., have stated as clearly as the main copy on that form, that you will do this, (or asked those signing to tick a request box for membership information)
- can record the data accurately
- are able to adequately protect that data, and will not keep it for an unreasonably long time
- can prevent casual passers-by reading such data off the screens of authorised users
- can ensure only authorised users in your organisation access such data
- delete files when they are no longer relevant (and know just when this is).

To thoroughly understand the requirements, you need to have a good knowledge of the Guidelines which are quite comprehensive. It is apparent, however, that some elements have not been thought through and others are not keeping up with the changing pace of technology.

It is in the public's and the NGO's interest for mailings to be as exactly targeted as possible, yet some of the guidelines seek to restrict the information held so that organisations are obliged to mail many more people than is necessary. Building up large amounts of information on donors enables their needs to be closely catered for, yet the direction and tenor of the guidelines is against this. If you engage in reciprocal mailings you are advised to state this and seek permission from all donors or members at the point at which they join the organisation. To do this would clearly make it impossibly expensive for many organisations to recruit through newspaper advertising, and would affect all other recruitment methods. A more sensible approach would have been to acknowledge that receiving information from like minded organisations is part and parcel of being a member or donor in the 90s. This would also avoid countless other individuals receiving letters that are inappropriate and enables charities to grow cost-effectively.

Today, many homes are equipped with computers linked to the Internet with email facilities and databases on CD-ROMs. Thousands of people may be in breach of the Act as they build up lists of names and addresses and process them for a variety of business related purposes.

There are, however, some exceptions to the Act and registration may not be necessary where personal data are:

- held in connection with personal, family or household affairs or for recreational use
- used only for preparing the text of documents
- used for calculating wages and pensions, keeping accounts or keeping records of purchases and sales for accounting purposes only
- used for distributing articles or information to data subjects
- held by a sports or recreational club which is not a limited company.

In relation to the final two points, data subjects must be asked if they object to the use of their details. You have been warned! Check Guideline 6 carefully if you intend to rely on an exception.

At the end of the day, the Guidelines are only the Registrar's view of the Act and not a substitute for it. Your own view may be equally correct until a precedent is established through a court case, of which there have been a number already.

Europe-wide legislation has been in the process of development for a long period of time and though, in its original form, it would initially have seriously damaged many NGOs' viability through its very restrictive nature, it has gradually been improved and may be useful in its final form.

Handling complaints

Complaints arrive well ahead of money, often by phone. It is important that people in the organisation know this, or your appeals will have a bad reputation early on. This is hard to shake, even if they become very successful financially. Keep your switchboard, press office and mail-opening room informed, so that they can deal professionally with taking calls, handling complaints and passing them on to be dealt with by the right person - usually you!

Always be ready to apologise and explain. Your members will understand, if you are prompt and courteous. Naturally, if you have made an error, do apologise and give a full explanation of how it came about. Someone who complains and is dealt with satisfactorily will often become a more convinced supporter than before.

Occasionally, you will have letters from people who are obviously bigoted, or incorrect in what they say, or who feel they have a genuine case for complaint when you have done nothing wrong. In these cases you can do no more than state your case clearly and simply. You may feel that you can never convince that person you are right, but you should always reply courteously.

Letters that are rude or offensive go straight in the bin, though sometimes they can be very funny. Do not make an issue of these or try to reply, unless you want to receive another.

More difficult to handle are letters from the seriously disturbed, that start out just slightly odd, but by the second or third letter are manifestly deranged. Again, this correspondence must be brought firmly to a close by clearly stating your case, and saying that you do not want any further correspondence on the subject. You may choose to reply one last time, stating that you will not reply to any further letters, but it is best to stop as soon as possible. Such correspondence can be very time consuming and distract you from your real goals. Often, such correspondents will write to several people in the organisation, keeping long pointless exchanges going indefinitely. It is best if one person takes over all answers and brings them to an end.

Acceptance of funds

The acceptance of funds with an easy conscience is all about preparation. Most fundraising organisations have evolved a set of guidelines for their fundraising operation. This will prevent its work being hindered and make it clear just what, and who, the organisation can accept from, before the asking is done. Doing this before you ask for funds saves an enormous amount of time and trouble later. Imagine your chagrin when your Executive Committee decides that a cheque for £50,000 from a major company must be returned, because a subsidiary of theirs in Ireland doesn't allow unions in their factory.

The rationale behind most guidelines is to permit the maximum income acquisition possible, without undermining the mission of the organisation.

Some organisations say they will accept any funds without strings attached to them, and if the funds come from those they work against, so much the better. However, you may like to consider that PR companies advise such businesses that setting up a large charitable fund is an effective way to influence the public and to let themselves be seen in a good light.

Guidelines are, however, notoriously difficult to construct in such a way that fundraising is not inadvertently crippled. A policy on accepting funds from companies may simply say, 'We will accept no funds from any company which harms the environment'. This statement will then need extensive qualification to deal with the interlinking of companies through the structure of multinationals, the raw material supply and product delivery companies. The obvious questions are, 'What exactly constitutes harm?' and, 'What about a company that is making great progress, should it be encouraged ?' Faced with that sort of guideline, it is tempting to give up on companies altogether. Similar problems come from over-simplistic guidelines on the arms trade, tobacco companies and those who have links with impoverished countries or repressive governments.

Some organisations, like the Campaign Against the Arms Trade, can provide a detailed and lengthy blacklist. Any such list, covering a fair range of ethical issues in even a fairly straightforward way, will include most companies. It may appear easier to say who you could accept money from, if it were not for the fact that there are no perfect companies in this imperfect world. Some, however, are struggling to improve, and it can help to recognise this in the manner of many ethical investment trusts. Unfortunately, those that might appear on such a list today could disappear tomorrow, thus undermining the cast-iron list approach.

Another, more flexible concept, is to say you will accept no funds from a source that would lower your organisation's standing in the eyes of the public, and then let each case be judged on its merits by the recipient body of your organisation, (which can raise any questions it may have to a higher level of your organisation for advice).

This is largely a question of empowerment and trust in the common sense of each separate part of your operation, (which for most organisations will simply be the head office). Until case histories have accrued, however, it may be sensible to mitigate such freedom with an approvals procedure for requests for donations over a certain level, and from any particular industry with which you are at odds.

Some organisations impose a percentage limit to prevent large donors from appearing to control the organisation. No more than ten percent of gross income is common, this is impractical for small organisations with a very low gross income - where will the first donation come from? This form of control also runs into problems when a capital appeal for, say, a new building, is contemplated. Here the early donations, which will be large, will often dwarf the normal gross income and the building may not succeed without those large donations. So, a method needs to exist whereby rules on acceptance of funds can be mitigated to suit the organisation's real needs and objectives.

Other organisations say simply, 'All funds are welcome but not earmarked for any specific project'. This is often found in large membership organisations where there are few funds from Trusts. If you wish to increase your Trust fundraising, this rule would be crippling, as Trusts like to sponsor discrete projects. It also raises another problem, in that membership organisations making frequent appeals for funds will cite different reasons for each appeal, and will need to make very clear to donors that their money is going into the general pot if that is indeed the case.

Many organisations welcome donations for specific projects and deliberately carve up their work into such projects. This makes fundraising easier and brings the donors much closer to the work of the organisation, making repeat gifts more likely.

Acceptance of funds policy

So, what is to be done? Each organisation needs to take time to consider the questions cited above in the light of the overall framework of maximising income, without damaging the work it is doing. As a fundraiser, it is in your interest to draft an *'Acceptance of Funds'* document, and ensure it passes through the relevant committees before you begin fundraising. Ask other organisations in your field for copies of their Code of Practice to help you, and to bring out all the issues for discussion, so that the debate does not occur year after year, as executive members think of new ethical issues to consider.

10 Future Developments

Interactive TV

Soon, it is said, we will all be shopping in the comfort of our own homes by the convenience of interactive TV. All we will need to do is flip to the shopping channels, select our goods, and feed in our credit card number for rapid delivery. That is, if we can tear ourselves away for long enough from the interactive game shows where we can win a million pounds, or the interactive soaps, where our choice will determine who marries whom and what happens next.

The communications superhighway is getting closer by the day and will revolutionise charity giving. If you a see a dreadful situation on TV, you will be able to help straight away by sending a credit card donation that minute to an appropriate charity, and by the end of the programme see help arrive with your name or company logo plastered all over it. If you are feeling charitable at the end of the month, (shortly after pay day), you will be able to search through a series of charity commercials and donate to whoever you like, instantly, effortlessly, and with the full knowledge of millions of other viewers, if you so wish.

The organisations that benefit from this will be those that have mastered the art of projecting their concerns on television. Those that fail will be those that do not have the resources or the imagination.

Making television work for charities

Currently, not many organisations can make television work for them, and very few are even experimenting with moving images and concepts. Many have had their fingers burnt by allowing advertising agencies to overrule their common sense. No one would today allow an agency to place an advertisement in a newspaper without a coupon, (though some agencies still try); but when it comes to television we are no longer on safe ground. We may feel sure that the commercial should have had a telephone number on it all the way through, and a voice saying 'Call the number right now', but we do not like to say so. Somehow it gets tacked, reluctantly, on the end, (not to spoil the creative effort), and our press advertising is supposed to benefit mysteriously from the prestige of our charity being seen on TV.

Just as fundraisers have learnt to control advertising agencies over press work, we will need to learn the tricks of our trade over TV commercials, and insist on the most effective direct response methods being used, with no concessions to raising the profile or winning awards. If the commercial works in raising funds, it will win those awards anyway.

Survival of the fittest

When it starts for real, the first few to become established will build up a learning curve that will be very hard to catch. Mistakes will be very costly and the barriers to entry of new participants will be high. Competition between organisations with the same theme will be cut-throat, as huge amounts of money will flow to those who are successful: and that could impoverish those who are not.

Good concepts will become the hallmark of certain charities. If Friends of the Earth were to use birds as their theme, how would that affect the RSPB ?

Direct Response Television (DRTV)

Already, there is a lot of practical information for organisations wishing to advertise on television. This has come from tests and trials in the UK and USA for home shopping and for charities. Assuming that you are seeking a direct response from a telephone number placed on the screen during your commercial, to be at all successful you will need an agency to handle the response. There are several good agencies now with relevant experience. British Telecom itself has agency facilities and if you are going to put on a telethon or a spectacular where the response will be huge, you must discuss it with them beforehand, as thousands of calls can be generated in a very short period.

The secret of DRTV

The secret of successful direct response commercials is your ability to handle the volume of calls generated. For years many more calls were lost than received, as lines jammed and people could not get through. Well equipped agencies can capture a much higher percentage of calls than ever before, transforming events. In some regions, DRTV accounts for 20% of TV advertisements and that figure is growing rapidly. A good agency will record all call details carefully and switch to a recorded service if calls begin to go over their capacity.

Call capture is the name of the game. You may wish just for an automated service but live operators can check details and begin to build a relationship. Talk through their scripts very carefully and ask people outside the organisation to let you know what they would think of such responses. Call capture must be quick, efficient and very polite. Your agency will need to know if your target is money or list building, what kind of people are likely to call, what questions they might ask, and how many calls that could be generated. This is very difficult to estimate the first time around.

The BBC's Children in Need programme resulted in 200,000 calls via Local 0345 numbers (charged at local rate). These were handled by 1,750 operators in over 50 centres. It successfully raised £17M. Incidentally, the call rates are changing and you will need to select the appropriate rate for your situation which may well not be Freephone. You must arrange with British Telecom how these calls will be charged and paid for. The options range from Freephone 0800 to premium lines on which the caller pays the maximum rate for the call.

For most fundraisers, that sort of mass appeal is an unlikely occurrence, (coming perhaps once in a lifetime), and you will have to buy your time on television instead. This is the big stumbling block as it is very expensive, but DRTV is said to work best outside peak times and to a selected audience. That is why Cable and Satellite networks attract a lot of DRTV. You will still need to keep the budget low and it is certainly not necessary to have a lavish creative spend. In fact, it is probably counter-productive. You will need to discover which channels your target audience watch, and when. Test out your ideas as cheaply as possible, ie. , on as small a scale as possible. You will also need to let your audience relate to you simply and emotively, so beware of pressure from your agency to adopt an intellectual or complex approach.

A classic campaign

You may well remember the NSPCC 'Ellie' campaign. If you can obtain a copy, view it several times. and then look at a typical commercial break and at other DRTV ads. Only when you have fully understood the difference between commercial advertising and successful DRTV appeals should you begin to think about using this medium. If in the eyes of the general public your charity answers a real need, you're in a position to create a successful TV appeal. If, however, you feel you cannot make the public share your perception of the importance of your organisation's work, perhaps a TV appeal will not meet your charity's needs. And if you do not feel that your charity's work is very important, perhaps you should change your job.

In any case, you will have to think about the appeal commercial from the point of view of your donors. Why do they give to you? What do they see in their mind's eye when they make out a cheque to you?

Think Timing for TV

Timing is very important. It is a factor you probably have not needed to think about in other fundraising media. You will need as long as it takes to put over your message and bring people to act. Any longer and people will turn off. It is worth experimenting with a 30 second commercial at the start of a break and 10 seconds at the end, for those who did not have their pens handy. Thinking in seconds can also improve the rest of your fundraising work. If you can't say it on the back of a bookmark you need a better copywriter. (But a great copywriter holding the reader for a full page will bring amazing results!)

People are not going to stand up and phone you unless you tell them to very clearly. Use a strong call to action - 'Phone us now...Pick up the phone and call now. Please don't wait to call...We are waiting for your call now...' Part of that clarity is having the phone number legible. It is recommended that it is at least two inches high and in the centre, middle or centre bottom of the screen in a colour that will stand out from the screen, preferably steady, ie. , not flashing. An easily remembered number helps a lot.

It is always useful to signal clearly that this advertisement will ask for a response. Do not surprise your audience. Whilst they are getting over the shock, the time for action will have passed. Let them feel they want to respond, not that they are being pushed into calling you. As in all response devices, let the viewer know just how much you are asking for and let them know what you will do with this sum if at all possible.

Remember that you are really after repeat business, rather than the maximum amount of money on the night. The number of people who have made a donation is more important than the total amount. If you are going to work with your favourite advertising agency, choose the specialist teams who understand direct mail. Never go for prestige advertising. It will cost you a great deal for very little response.

Responding to demographic trends

Age may play an important part, as younger professionals give to their causes through TV and older viewers stay with press ads and direct mail. This means that charities have to keep a very careful check on their supporters' age profile, to avoid being wiped out as the age of those using TV to give rises inexorably. Conversely, fundraisers may need to segment their appeals with care. Do you advertise for legacies on TV, to get into the wills of young professionals, or do you advertise in the press to reach the older generation? Can you afford to do both? We could be entering a very uncertain era, where the old adage of 'test, test and test again' becomes the most important touchstone of our efforts.

The Internet

Likewise, the more purely interactive regions of global network computers and the Internet may offer untold possibilities. On the simplest level, as governments and companies end the pleasant anarchy of the Internet and turn it commercial, we are becoming more able to learn of problems around the world, through bulletin boards and World Wide Web sites, for which donations can be made by credit card. The next stage could be donations given via a special charity credit card that an intermediate organisation, (card agency), will hold an account for, only paying to charities that give proof of validity. This could be rather like a CAF voucher, but claimed by the charity from the agency after some charity credential checking to limit fraud, or paid by the agency to the charity on your instructions.

Virtual reality may one day offer donors the possibility of entering the restricted world of disabled people or see hardship through the eyes of a child. Affinity for the suffering of individuals could be literal. The phrase, 'If you were in their place you would think differently,' could be put to the test. In a world where it is easy to insulate yourself from human problems, virtual reality could be profoundly moving and resensitise people whose conscience has been deadened by pervasive materialism.

The Internet currently offers at least three useful possibilities for fundraisers. It is an immense information resource that can provide you with background information on countries, businesses, events, news, etc. The amount of available information is growing rapidly.

At the time of writing it is an interesting, but usually slow way to acquire such knowledge. Specialist fundraising sites that offer lists of trusts and foundations, for example, have just begun to appear. However, new sites are being added at a phenomenal rate and the tools for locating such sites, are also growing in sophistication. The Internet also provides a powerful tool to link to other fundraisers around the world. If you are already connected to an email system you will appreciate the ease of communication that it affords.

Within international organisations, email provides a very rapid and straightforward way to communicate across time zones and physical distance. Given a person's email address, you can send messages to them wherever their computer is located. As email can also be sent and received via many laptop computers, this can often be wherever their laptop happens to be in the world. If, for example, you are visiting alumni prospects in Seoul and need information on a person or company in bulk, then this can be taken from a colleague's computer files in Edinburgh and enclosed with the reply to your email message directly to your laptop, where you can read on screen or print out or update the information.

Given the nine hour time difference, your message can be sent from, say, your hotel room in the evening at 21.00 hrs, when it will be 13.00 hrs in your office in Edinburgh. That gives a whole afternoon for information to be compiled, which you can pick up first thing in the morning before you start work the next day.

If you are working for an organisation where there are several fundraisers in the country or world-wide, they can be linked by email in a discussion or information forum which people can add to at an appropriate time for them. There are also several such open forums which you can join now. You can join them via UK Fundraising (see below). It is best to be a passive listener for a while until you know the appropriate form for your interventions in any such discussion. Discussion groups have their own netiquette.

Fundraising sites on the Internet

Moving from simple email to the World Wide Web, the first site specifically set up to provide fundraisers with information is called UK Fundraising which can be found on http://www.fundraising.co.uk. This was created by Howard Lake as part of an MSc research project, and is an excellent site which is well maintained. (Incidentally, Howard Lake can also be reached by email on bh543@city.ac.uk). From that site it is possible to travel to many other fundraising-related sites, offering information on a range of topics from current fundraising vacancies to fundraising software, to Greenpeace's fundraising site, and to Cooking on the Net, a fundraising project designed to help fund organisations who connect underprivileged children with computer resources.

For an up-to-date guide to useful sites on the Internet (and much more), I recommend Howard Lake's book 'Fundraising on the Internet' (Aurelian 1996). Howard declares that 'despite the attractions of the World Wide Web, the most successful fundraising will be carried out via email.' He also recommends fully integrating your World Wide Web site with programme work as well as your fundraising initiatives for maximum effect.

Raising funds on the Internet

There are many organisations now doing this from their own Web sites. Mostly they use Internet equivalents of ordinary fundraising techniques. Membership organisations have a simple coupon one can fill in and email back to the organisation. The fee is then either paid by the usual methods such as cheque through the post, or a credit card number is given. Some sites warn that this is no more safe than any usual email communication. There are now, however, increasingly secure ways of giving credit card details. This makes donating much easier, so it is important that you consider the most secure method available when you come to set up your own site. There are now many commercial sites on the Internet and you can buy virtually anything through those sites. More interesting ideas involve treasure hunts through the net, virtual world tour concerts where the donor can hear their favourite groups play just for them, and email appeals like Plugged In (http://www.pluggedin.org/).

Try also:

Friends of the Earth http://www.foe.co.uk

Amnesty International http://www.io.org/amnesty (which is one of some dozen sites world-wide)

Setting up your WWW site

The best way to understand what kind of site is possible is to research everyone else's first and select the best method for presenting your own information. It is important to understand that marketing on the Net is different from standard marketing. To have people visit your site you need to drum up business by letting everyone who might be interested know where it is. One way to do that is to join the discussion groups that your potential customers might be interested in. Advertising yourself in an obvious way is not acceptable—this should only be done when it is appropriate in the conversation. And remember, links to your site from other sites help enormously. Most sites have highlighted text that you can click on to reach a new but related site: the more chances there are of that happening the better. It is a normal method of browsing which suits the Net environment. Naturally, you will want to let all your supporters know, and everyone else, that you can be reached through conventional means, but the new world of the Net has at least 50,000,000 inhabitants who are usually affluent and well educated, so reaching them effectively will be important. Increasingly, donors are coming to expect a URL (Internet address) to be included in publicity material.

Secondly, repeat business comes through having an interesting site. The interactive process for most sites is that information is given, questions are answered: as much interactivity as possible is the glue that keeps customers. If your site is interesting they will come back; if it is boring there are plenty more sites to visit. For more technical details look at CommerceNet (http://www.commerce.net) which is a not-for-profit consortium that supplies high technology product information, secure ways of ordering and payment facilities. Also look at Open Market commercial sites through http://www.directory.net. This is a free service that can be browsed either by keyword or alphabetically. In constructing a site, remember that few people have fast modems, so large colour illustrations, that take a long time to download, can cause your visitor to cancel their visit before they have seen your picture. Alternatively, you can provide them with text or images, including short sequences of motion video, that they can download and view at their leisure. Large providers of on-line services are getting slower to get through to as they attract thousands more customers, so speed of delivery is currently becoming more important.

How much money will I make?

Right now there are no hard statistics but though most sites are not goldmines they are certainly attracting new members and donors in limited numbers and repaying the time and effort that have gone into building them. The sites are so new that it is too early to know the volume of repeat business or the quality of those joining. In some ways, this is just a forerunner to the super-communications highway which could lead consumers to change their buying habits and order goods and services through their televisions with ease and efficiency. If so, then those organisations that have learnt to handle the Net may be ahead of the game. It is entirely possible, however, that such a highway may have much more in common with Direct Response TV than the Net.

Bar-coding

As a fundraiser, I am deeply fascinated by supermarkets' checkout tills, with such huge amounts of money passing through such a small space so quickly.

- Why not introduce your organisation's leaflet next to all those tills, with a simple bold appeal and a bar-code so that donations can be rung up? £5 to 'Save the Snails' would appear on your grocery bill alongside your cabbage, etc., and at the end of the month the chain of stores would pay a huge sum into your organisation's bank account.

- Of course, bar-codes have many uses. Your organisation's membership card could have a bar-code on it so that your members, too, could give £5 every time they shopped; and when they took part in your AGM they could be booked in, out, and vote, all by means of their card. They could also use the card to pay reduced fees on a large range of products. It might even reduce your membership drop out rate considerably.

- Bar-codes could also reduce your processing time and cost for appeals. Next to each address on the coupon a bar-code could be read, instead of the membership number being entered or the whole name and address being typed into your database.

The Post Office should not be far behind in being able to deliver letters by means of bar codes. This would mean much greater accuracy for deliveries and for your database memory.

Bar-code readers are relatively inexpensive and their speed and accuracy are very high. The only current limitation on their use is your imagination. Eventually, they will be used by all charities - but you can steal a march on them and move up the learning curve by investing in the technology now.

Psychographics

An interesting development in targeted direct mail has been submerged in the direct mail recession, but can be of great interest to fundraisers looking to broaden the membership of their organisations.

Different people respond to different approaches

Psychographics assumes that people have a range of different psychological views of the world and different ways of relating to it, and so need approaching in a way that corresponds to their individual psychology.

For example, if you are raising funds for sheltered accommodation for elderly people, you might be using mailing lists which include those who are very patriotic, those who are very international, those who are very self-centred, and those who are altruistic. Each of these people will react differently to the emphasis in your message, so it is prudent to put your message in language that the people will take in.

Identifying the differences ...

In order to tell which people on your mailing list fall into which categories, a free offer is often used. This is on the lines of 'If you send for more information you will receive a free gift. Kindly tick the box for the gift you require.' The gifts could be tea-towels with the flag of your country, or a map of the world, a scarf, or a book-token sent on their behalf to a friend. Obviously, this will not be a foolproof system, and you can, no doubt, find better and more appropriate examples of gifts than mine.

... and the advantages of knowing about them

This exercise will, however, enable you to approach your audience with a much better chance of speaking their language. It will also solve several problems for you. For example, should you mention that a large proportion of the people you will be helping are ex-service men, or do you feature the multi-racial aspect of your work, or do you emphasise that the donor's name will appear on a plaque on the wall of the building, or that a tree will be planted for every donation given?

This technique takes some time and trouble to think through and get right, but it is especially useful if you are raising a limited amount of large donations. The cost of issuing four different letters could be easily repaid. It also pays to tailor your letter in a similar way to different mailing lists, all of them addressing different psychologies. (And shouldn't you be writing rather different appeal letters to men and women, to old and young supporters?)

Of course, your psychographics cannot just stop at the acquisition stage. It is equally important to follow this through by recognising people's differences in the rest of your communications. With high-value donors this can be very rewarding over their lifetime with you.

Changes in the law

In common with many other Western governments, our current Conservative government has, within limits, pursued a policy of state withdrawal from expenditure on the provision of social services, and has looked for a parallel, though not equivalent, strengthening of the work of the voluntary sector.

As part of that strengthening, it has been made progressively easier for charities to claim back the tax that donors have paid on various donations. Other changes are to be expected, and a careful eye needs to be kept on all such government moves. This is professionally undertaken by the ICFM and NCVO on behalf of philanthropic organisations, but it is essential for all fundraisers to know exactly how the law is interpreted on each fundraising activity, and to keep abreast of all new developments. Fundraisers and finance officers need to be particularly vigilant over VAT, which is currently being collected with almost religious zeal from almost every possible charitable transaction.

The Charities Act 1992

The Charities Act 1992 is particularly far-reaching, and you should be familiar with its implications. It covers three areas of fundraising:

- the employment of fundraising agents and agencies
- the reporting of financial details to the Charity Commission
- the control of public charitable collections (basically door-to-door and flag day collections).

The idea is to protect the public from fraud as far as possible, to make charities more accountable, and to regulate the growing number of collections. It is stressed that, 'the Government fully supports responsible fund-raising for good charitable causes.' Some controls are, however, felt to be essential. A balance is therefore to be struck between enabling and regulating charitable fundraising.

Interestingly, this legislation was held up whilst the Deregulation Task Force's views were being formed. This was the eighth Deregulation Task Force, set up in September 1993, to look specifically at charities and voluntary organisations, (the other seven having been business Task Forces). The current proposals for legislation take into account discussions between the Home Office and the Task Force.

Proposed legislation

We should note, on the positive side, that proposals for legislation increasingly talk about charities 'and organisations with philanthropic purposes,' in the same breath. However, this is not always followed up in the same spirit in subsequent legislation.

For example, such non-charitable but philanthropic organisations will be disadvantaged as the granting of national exemptions from the requirement for local authority permission to hold street collection passed from the Home Office to the Charity Commissioners, (who will only deal with registered charities). Consequently, such organisations will need to apply for permission to every local authority in whose area they wish to collect. This will greatly add to the burden of work by both NGOs and local authorities, and make it exceedingly difficult to co-ordinate collections across the country effectively - if, indeed, this will still be possible. The costs of such collections will thus be greatly increased.

In drafting new legislation, the Government has, however, also sought the advice of charities, appropriate individuals and organisations through documents such as the consultation document issued by the Home Office Voluntary Service Unit on public charitable collections (Part II of the 1992 Act). This is part of an ongoing consultation process that is being carried out as this significant piece of legislation is shaped and put into practice. The ICFM has followed this closely and represented the interests of professional fundraisers, informing them as developments have taken place.

Predicting the future

Unfortunately this is rarely possible with any degree of certainty, but the rapidly changing external environment in which we work makes it essential for us to keep a watchful eye on trends in fundraising. In business it is often the second company to move into a new field which maximises its income rather than the initial trailblazer, but it is rarely the last few to change who benefit. One area that has quietly been gathering steam is fundraising outside the West, particularly in the Asia Pacific countries. The next chapter looks at overseas fundraising, and identifies some interesting possibilities.

11 Fundraising in Other Countries

Money from overseas

The key source of overseas funds for work in the UK is the EU, which is dealt with in Chapter 6. Technically, there are a variety of overseas foundations which could support projects in the UK. *The International Foundation Directory* (Europa Publications. Consultant Editor H V Hodson) gives a good flavour of what is available, as does the *Directory of Organisations concerned with Peace and Security*. There is also a huge directory of American foundations called *The Foundation Directory*, published by The Foundation Centre, New York, which could contain some useful addresses, but you should not take the trouble unless you have exhausted all the possible UK sources of funds and feel that your work is foundation friendly, and you have someone knowledgeable to undertake the spadework for you. It is also quicker to check in *US Foundation Support in Europe 1994/5* edited by Ruth Lauer & Steve England, published by the Directory of Social Change.

If you do need to look further, the Charities Aid Foundation has a collection of US Foundation literature at its London Offices. If you work for an international organisation with branches or projects overseas, you may be well placed to tap not only the UK market, but also foundations and organisations in other countries, to fund those branches or projects. In many instances, it may be more effective for you to assist them to submit the final application themselves. For example, your Eastern European branch in Hungary may be totally inexperienced in approaching foundations, and yet the local Soros Foundation may wish to fund just the kind of work that they undertake. For applications involving more than one country, it may be preferable for you to approach their offices in London or New York, but the application will succeed, more usually, if you assist your local branch to develop the skills necessary to place a successful application, carry out the work, evaluate it, and report back on progress in meeting objectives.

Many international organisations either have branches in other countries that are dependent on them for financial support, or fund projects in other countries, never suspecting that they may well be able to raise their own funds locally, thus enabling the local branch to achieve a degree of financial and political independence. In most developed 'western' countries there is a healthy fundraising culture with professional fundraisers and fundraising conferences and workshops at which skills can be learnt and exchanged. Most advanced are the USA, Canada, Australia, South Africa and Europe. In Europe, the principal fundraising event of the year is the International Fundraising Workshop at Nordwijkerhout in the Netherlands, in October. Started in 1981, the Workshop has become an annual three day event which, in 1993, had more than 500 participants from 31 countries and from all continents. It is run by the International Fund Raising Group (a non-profit making trust) which, in 1991, set up a permanent secretariat in London. (International Fund Raising Workshops Ltd. 295 Kennington Road, London SE11 4QE. Tel: +44 (0)71 587 0287, Fax: +44 (0)71 582 4335).

International workshops

In the past few years a flourishing and rapidly expanding international programme of workshops has been set up. Workshops have been held in many countries including India, Mexico, Zimbabwe and Hong Kong. Many more are planned giving comprehensive global coverage.

International organisations like the World Wide Fund for Nature (WWF), HelpAge International, Greenpeace, Oxfam and Amnesty International are sending their overseas staff and partners to these workshops and are often running additional internal workshops to facilitate fundraising in all the countries in which they operate. This has come about because of a gradual realisation that every country has a relatively rich, educated, middle class who are used to giving to religions and political parties (both of which run very sophisticated fundraising programmes in nearly every country).

These people are also linked by the same communications media of sophisticated newspapers, television and radio. They share the same aspirations and an increasingly similar culture which paves the way for them to participate in philanthropy. Those organisations that have understood the potential, (eg. there are over 100 million middle class people in India), are frequently operating in a competition-free environment. Techniques such as direct mail and advertising are hardly used by NGOs outside the West, yet they can bring huge rewards.

Fundraising in India

Some years ago I worked in India for Mr K. S. Gupta for Lok Kalyan Samiti (LKS), a Delhi based family and medical welfare charity which specialises in is eye operations. For a long time he has been running a sophisticated and very profitable fundraising campaign. His newspaper advertisements ask the reader to save one person's eyesight by sending LKS the equivalent of £5 in rupees, in return for which they receive a photograph of the person whose eyesight they have saved. As LKS then has the name and address of the person who gave, we then wrote to them at the time of various festivals, with a message such as, 'This is Holi, the festival of colour. Blind people can see no colours. Please be generous again and sponsor the rebirth of light for 2, 4, or 6 people', 'This is Diwali, the Festival of Light ...', 'This is Independence Day, blind people have no independence...'

This has been repeated several times a year. Not only is this simple system effective, but variations and new ideas are tried out constantly. Newspaper editors were approached for free space, (using an important newspaper contact who first gave free space himself), which resulted in many free advertisements across India. This meant that the advertisements needed to be translated in several languages and the picture of a person with bandaged eyes had to be changed to suit the various newspapers' readerships (a Sikh for Sikh newspapers etc.).

Direct mail lists were not available and so other ideas were tested. Telephone directories were tried because most people with a phone would be reasonably well off and would have been in the same house for about four years. Their address would often reflect their occupation. Residents' associations were approached to use their newsletters, especially in areas where teachers or other caring professionals were known to live. Company contacts were tapped for their client lists. The 'Who's Who' of India was mailed for celebrity support, and every contact with LKS was placed on the mailing list.

The expansion of names and addresses was such that before long the whole system needed computerising. Now LKS has many thousands of donors across the country. Naturally, a newsletter is sent to each donor and new ideas are tested there too. For example, birthdays and remembrance days are popular. The newsletter also lets people know much more about the organisation they support and there is a set invitation to visit LKS and see the work in progress.

LKS has been able to tell some European development agencies that it could now manage without their assistance and it has been an inspiration to other NGOs on the sub continent. Many other organisations are also effectively fundraising in India. Examples include the children's organisation CRY India, Aide et Action and HelpAge International, which has for many years run thousands of sponsored walks in schools, and which has over the past few years branched out into many other activities including an impressive Art Auction. All these and many more agencies are now assisting with the running of annual fundraising workshops in India which can teach any NGO dozens of new ideas.

Fundraising in South America

Peru

The economy of Peru has been devastated by a long civil war and the horrors of massive international debt. Many people feel that they have dropped rapidly down the class structure in the past few years. NGOs are often substantially funded from abroad though most are also engaged in a degree of fundraising locally. The techniques of fundraising are often similar to those used in Europe. For example, the Peruvian Foundation for the Conservation of Nature was the most advanced and impressive fundraising organisation I visited. Trained in Canada, their fundraiser has raised substantial sums from top business people by organising seminars, dinners and meetings at which they are personally targeted as individuals. She also raises funds through direct mail to lists in the USA, though direct mail in Peru has not worked for her and events have not been as successful as expected.

Chile

Here, by contrast, the professional classes are feeling well off and the country has an air of successful economic and social progress. Two of the many organisations that raise funds locally are Compartiendo La Mesa and the Hogar de Cristo. Both their Directors are impressive fundraisers working with relatively small organisations and developing their own approaches to fundraising. Their work is very similar to the work being done by kindred organisations in Europe. Door to door collections, by large numbers of volunteers, of relatively small amounts of money on a regular basis, give an echo of various schemes in England. Dinners with celebrities are popular and trading goods and other promotional items help to give a positive image of the organisation. Art auctions, street collections and concerts have also been held in Chile.

Venezuela

The days of very rapid development of the Venezuelan economy are over. Now, with the attempted coup d'état in 1992 and increasing social instability, the professional classes are less sure of their disposable income, but there is still a great deal that can be done as the country is relatively wealthy. Bioma, an environmental organisation specialising in protected 'park' areas is expanding its local income at a great rate. Likewise, ANAPACE, (a charity dealing with cerebral palsy), are making large sums from all the classic western donor-base fundraising techniques. Organisations which cater for a problem that does not distinguish between rich and poor, (such as diseases like cancer), are well placed to run basic donor pyramid-based fundraising operations. They can be sure that a reasonable number of wealthy people have been affected or know of other people who have been affected.

These people are the ideal target group as they have both knowledge and disposable income. Often the donor-base grows out of a simple victim support organisation offering advice and/or assistance to those affected and their families. From this base a more substantial operation can grow, but this is a major step to take and will require a larger investment for much smaller returns than the early days. The organisation would do well to realise that it is moving into a new era, and that it will have to resource and support that move steadfastly until the expected returns kick in.

Fundraising in the former Soviet Union

Until recently, philanthropy has been a state concern and collections were taken in the workplace, (the hub of Soviet life), for various charitable endeavours. 'If part of a co-operative's income (profit) is donated to the Lenin Soviet Children's Fund, the Soviet Peace Fund or the Cultural Foundation of the USSR, or used for other charitable purposes, it shall not be subject to taxation.' This is a quote from the Draft Law, 'On Co-operative Economy in the USSR', which makes an interesting contrast to the basic definitions of charity and philanthropy once current in Soviet society.

'CHARITY. Aid hypocritically rendered by representatives of the ruling class in an exploiter society to a part of the poor population in order to deceive the workers and divert them from the class struggle.' *Great Soviet Encyclopaedia 1950.*

'PHILANTHROPY. Bourgeois charity, aid to, and protection for the poor.' *Dictionary of the Russian Language 1987.*

As the pace of change quickens, new fundraising ventures are evolving. Concerts are held to raise money for drug addicts, street stalls raise funds for the miners, lotteries are held, etc. One organisation recently active is The Soviet Peace Fund. Set up in 1961 and collecting public and private funds which are used to run international peace congresses, it helps the victims of war and aggression and those suffering from natural disasters. In 1987 it raised 273,400,000 roubles from tens of millions of people.

The Soviet Cultural Foundation, founded in 1987, is one of the most important philanthropic organisations. It organises benefit concerts, performances, sales and auctions for the restoration and protection of cultural monuments and to assist artists. The Lenin Soviet Children's Fund was also set up in 1987 to tackle the enormous problems in the child care field. One of its first tasks was the payment of 6 million roubles to cover teachers' salaries in orphanages.

Donors are by no means naive, as this letter to Izvestia in 1988, (quoted in *Philanthropy in the Soviet Society* by Vitali Tretyakov) shows. 'The workers at my factory were told to send one day's pay to the Peace Fund, but no one was very enthusiastic about doing this... The workers said openly the Peace Fund had an oversized bureaucratic staff, and it did not want to finance its members' trips abroad or pay their salaries. Why aren't reports on the Fund's spending regularly published by the press? At our meetings we decided to transfer our money to the Children's Fund, in particular to one specific children's home. Please understand that we don't grudge our money for concrete steps linked with the struggle for peace, and we are ready to help orphans and problem kids. There is no problem as far as the victims of the Chernobyl accident or natural disasters is concerned. But we have had enough of bureaucracy!' A. Chizov.

Does this sound familiar? Incidentally, by 1988 the Fund had twenty-three permanent staff members and their salaries were paid out of money earned by the fund itself and not from donations. As Eastern European societies have opened up, many international organisations have begun fundraising workshops and conferences. So far, these have had limited success. There is little in the way of financial resources to set up serious fundraising from scratch, entrepreneurs are not easy to find, (let alone in voluntary organisations), and staff and volunteers' circumstances change rapidly. There has also been the problem of 'looking expectantly to the West' rather than facing the less pleasant task of trying to raise money within crumbling dislocated societies. As, however, much of Eastern Europe becomes Central Europe and prosperity comes to some countries there will be increasing chances to raise funds for philanthropic causes.

Fundraising in Africa

Africa has a rich tradition of family philanthropy. Often as someone gains wealth their obligations to the wider family grow at the same rate. There are also the well trodden paths of political and religious fundraising. In many countries NGO fundraising has reached quite sophisticated levels.

Zimbabwe

In Zimbabwe, for example, even in 1989 the Salvation Army were using mailing list techniques, (and legacies were left to hospitals like St Giles', though few NGOs were seriously trying to raise such funds). The Rotary movement was using casinos set up in hotels to raise funds for specific charitable work (gambling was illegal unless for charitable purposes). Street collections were popular though the sums raised were not large. Charity concerts were often held in the largest venues, sometimes with international artists, and Christmas card sales, jumble sales and other sales of almost anything were also held.

Schools' fundraising was big business with much money going to help fund the schools themselves, for example, through sponsored bicycle rides. The late Sally Mugabe's Children's Fund was very active in schools. Their fundraising included an exciting sponsored dance marathon. Extensive schools' fundraising has also taken place for the Save The Rhinos Project with a goal of £1M, though there was apparently a shortfall from this target. Gifts in kind from industry are quite common. HelpAge Zimbabwe have received scrap cloth, reject enamel, tyres for their refugees programme, cement benches for one of their homes, etc. Industry and commerce give large sums to prestigious projects such as the Mayor of Bulawayo's fund or the Child Survival Programme because of the influence of their powerful patrons, but the business community has been heavily pressured by Government to contribute to many events and celebrations and has become rather resistant to lesser appeals.

Blocked funds

In some countries, the government does not allow foreign companies to repatriate their profits. Such profits are known as blocked funds. Blocked funds are often a major source of large scale donations but the results can also be quite small scale. If you have a branch or project in a country that has blocked the repatriation of currency to the UK, it is always worthwhile asking the DTI for a list of UK companies operating there and contacting them all, asking for them to release their profits to your charity. If some of them have helped you in the UK, this may open up the way to a serious donation in currency you can use but they cannot. If large sums and an American company are involved, try talking to the central bank in the country where you are operating, to see if they will release the funds to the UK for a brief period. The company can then offset the donation, (to a UK registered charity), against tax liabilities before returning the rest into the block within a strict time limit and paying a small fee to the central bank (say 2 or 3%). Or try suggesting half the blocked funds are used for charitable purposes in the country where they are blocked and the other half repatriated, (or some such variation of percentages).

If you are sending funds overseas, it is often more effective to send something like a tractor which can be readily sold for far more than it cost, (including shipping), to increase the funds you have available for your project. Do not forget the commercial disciplines of doing this. For example, poor countries are littered with tractors that have no spare parts so you should send at least two years' worth, or no one will buy your tractor. (The sale should, of course, have been arranged beforehand.)

In Zimbabwe there were some commercial ventures raising funds for charity. Jairos Jiri had two shops selling handicraft goods and the then Bulawayo Council for the Welfare of the Disabled, (now the National Council), had a model shop in Bulawayo selling clothes made on the premises by people with various disabilities. Embassies in most poor countries are a very useful source of funds and Zimbabwe is no exception. Though the sums available are not large by European standards they can make a very significant difference, as can the use of vehicles or a word from the ambassador to the right person.

From the above it can be seen that there are three fundraising sectors in the country. One, largely outlined above, is by organisations like Rotary, the Soroptimists and other NGOs. The second is political party fundraising and fundraising using the party network. This has been done very successfully, for example, by ZIMOFA (the Zimbabwe Mozambique Friendship Association) which had links to Zanu PF, the ruling party. The third sector is the Church and Mission fundraising which appears to be fairly undeveloped, being based on churches or missions meeting their own needs with little fundraising at a national level. Churches do occasionally undertake second collections, as they have done for both ZIMOFA and the Rhino Campaign.

Fundraising in Pacific Rim countries

The wealthy economies of the Pacific Rim countries have begun to attract the attention of several foreign NGOs, some of whom have been working for several years to build organisations capable of unlocking the huge wealth that has built up. Sometimes this has been merely fortuitous.

Oxfam in Hong Kong, for example, received a large legacy, some years ago, which prompted it to think of becoming more independent by raising funds locally. Now it runs a sophisticated system like any European NGO and raises a considerable sum each year. Hong Kong also has a famous flag day pitch and the few organisations that are fortunate enough to receive permission to fundraise there can be assured of a good return for their effort. It remains to be seen if this will continue after 1997 and indeed if the concept of an NGO will survive. Theoretically, no organisation that is a branch of a foreign NGO will be able to operate. All such organisations must become local under the Chinese basic law.

Japan, South Korea and Taiwan are obvious targets. They are rich countries with excellent communications systems and middle class lifestyles similar to those found almost everywhere in the world. There is little NGO fundraising of any scale as yet in Taiwan or Korea but Japan has many NGOs receiving funds from a variety of sources. Once registered as an organisation capable of receiving funds, it is possible to solicit gifts from industry, trusts and rich individuals who can be extraordinarily generous. Registration, however, is not easy: applicants are required to lodge several million yen in a bank account and follow a complicated legal procedure. In all these tiger countries there are trusts and foundations to which applications can be made. Often they have been set up by companies now staffed by young MBAs educated in America and Canada, who bring back the American business ethic to their home countries. Buddhist organisations, in particular, are both effective fundraisers and distributors of charities. The fastest growing local NGO in Taiwan is a Buddhist organisation that raises its funds by direct person to person contact, often in offices.

In the Pacific Rim, more so than in other parts of the world, fundraising is best done through your local organisation to avoid cultural gaffes. In beginning to introduce new fundraising ideas to your branch, be prepared for a long wait before you are 'accepted' and another wait before your ideas are fully considered, especially in Japan where decisions are made more collectively than in the West. Bear in mind that middle management is very important in Japanese companies. New ideas will certainly not be implemented until the relevant group in the NGO feels they are the right way to go. Full responsibility for decision-making is rarely given to individuals in Japanese companies but, once made, decisions will be put into effect quickly and efficiently.

As in most Far Eastern cultures, it is important not to put people on the spot. Remember it is far easier to elicit a polite, positive answer than a negative one. A little thought and sensitivity will usually make uncertain meanings clear. Asking questions that cannot be answered with a 'yes' or 'no' helps. One way of conveying 'no' in Japanese is to say something is 'difficult' but that does not necessarily mean the end of the affair. The word 'wakarimashita' is often translated as, 'I understand', but it means that you also agree. Asking for 'co-operation' means more than just trying hard. It means agreeing to do what is asked. Doing what is requested wins great appreciation in Japanese society and debts are repaid in due course. Patience in discussion is also rewarded and silences are not the negative experience they may be in the west.

At the moment direct mail is effective in Japan for commercial companies, despite the recession, as well as for NGOs. Greenpeace made good use of this technique when the environment was a popular local issue. Use hand written (calligraphed) envelopes to rich donors and trade on the loyalty they have to an organisation that they have taken the important step of joining. Trading goods also sell well, especially traditional items such as Christmas cards. T shirts are also popular, though few designs will travel effectively from Europe.

Two organisations that are designed to help businesses but can also provide useful information to NGOs, are JETRO, the Japanese External Trade Organisation, (a non-profit semi-governmental organisation from which some of the advice above is taken) and the Japan Business Consultancy (19 Somerset Place, Bath, BA1 5SF, Tel: 01225 444190)

Fundraising in the Middle East

In Islamic countries, mosques are places where funds can be solicited by the poor but fundraising as a professional activity is largely unknown and untested. Funds are usually raised on a personal basis from the very rich. With the polarisation of societies in North Africa, the creation of donor-based NGOs is difficult. For example, simply registering as an organisation can take many years if it happens at all.

Incidentally, in Israel, charitable funds have traditionally been sought from the West, but there are many local foundations and NGOs are developing sophisticated fundraising techniques.

§

It is my belief that many NGOs should be developing strategies based on globalising their operations, and as a key part of that process, evening out their income flows between the US, Europe and the Asia Pacific countries. In particular many NGOs could benefit in the medium- to long-term from serious investment in developing a donor-base in the tiger economies of the Pacific Rim.

12 Careers in Fundraising

Fundraising is one of the fastest-growing professions in the Western world. Fuelled by the withdrawal of government support from social services of all kinds and the growth of that part of the population that social scientists call 'inner directed', fundraising now provides one of the most interesting and worthwhile careers of the Nineties.

You will need to have an interest in marketing and in people's motivation for giving, as well as a desire to work in the 'charity' sector. An entrepreneurial attitude is essential, though the necessary skills can be acquired through training.

Career paths

If you are thinking of becoming a fundraiser, there are several possible routes to follow. Many years ago fundraising was considered a suitable occupation for aristocratic ladies with a social conscience or ex-army officers without one. The governing bodies of charitable organisations were filled with the great and the good, but today they are run by those elected by the grass-roots and the great and good are only allowed to put in an occasional appearance on such bodies as appeal committees (where they can be invaluable). So marrying into the aristocracy, joining the army or doing great service to your country are not now recommended routes to gaining employment as a fundraiser.

Today there are two main paths. The first is to work your way up inside an organisation, starting perhaps as a volunteer in the fundraising department (or sometimes as the volunteer fundraiser), and later obtaining paid employment with the same organisation. This will probably be enhanced by taking a series of courses from organisations like the Directory of Social Change or the Institute of Charity Fundraising Managers (ICFM). The other way is to work commercially acquiring an appropriate marketing skill such as direct mail, advertising, retailing or just business management. Then learning how to apply that skill in the voluntary sector - which can be a very daunting experience.

A hybrid version of these two paths is also beginning to develop with people acquiring the necessary skills by taking courses and then applying for fundraising positions with the charity of their choice. Needless to say, it is very difficult to build a successful career if you limit yourself to one organisation and career development usually involves moving from one voluntary organisation to another. The largest and most prestigious charities carry the most weight when it comes to assessing your record. On the other hand, with the withdrawal of government from all manner of social funding around the world, there is a dramatically increasing demand for fundraisers with a good track record. This is most keenly felt in the capital appeal field, with the need for large sums of money to finance new hospital buildings and the like.

Voluntary organisations are rarely the caring lifestyle workplace they aspire to be and can mirror some of the worst faults of the commercial world with staff displaying every trait from ruthless ambition to pigheaded incompetence. In general, however, their work is to a very high standard of efficiency and effectiveness which would be the envy of the commercial world if it realised just how well they are performing.

The volunteer's route

There are many levels of entry into fundraising. At the simplest, you can volunteer for work with almost any charity and the chances are you will be welcome to assist, though the fundraising department may not need help immediately, and you may have to begin somewhere else in the organisation, such as the campaigns, press, or office management departments.

Though this may seem very attractive from the outside, the principal work of volunteers is mundane and repetitive. There is never any guarantee of moving to paid work, though it does happen. When it happens, it tends to be because the volunteer either has skills the charity needs, or acquires a proficiency which is indispensable in an area where the charity wishes to expand. It is important to stress that many volunteers spend years doing virtually full-time jobs without ever having the chance of being paid.

Having worked as a volunteer in the organisation to which you are applying for a job, does, however, confer many advantages over someone from the outside or someone who has no experience of NGO work at all. You will rapidly learn a great deal about the inner workings of voluntary organisations and obtain a feel for the life. NGOs are not lifestyle organisations where the most enlightened social theories are practised, but are often stressed, under-resourced organisations, struggling to cope with the most serious problems of the age. Their commitment to being caring and consultative organisations, frequently degenerates into faction-fighting in which staff deploy all the campaigning skills they usually reserve for changing the world. But it must be said that charity work can also be extremely rewarding in a personal sense.

The organisation, for its part, will learn about the volunteer's capabilities at first hand rather than through the restrictive means of a CV and interview.

Volunteering as a first step can be done simply at local group level, where anyone interested in fundraising is often welcome and can pick up a great deal of practical experience. This is often, however, necessarily restricted in scope, dealing mainly with a variety of small events, trading from stalls and bringing in local membership fees. Local group work does offer many useful insights, both into an organisation you may be interested in working for, and into the psychology of giving, which will hold you in good stead in the future years of your career.

Local groups are often both the grass roots of national organisations and the democratic heart of those organisations. As such, they often elect regional representatives who sit on the voluntary council or board of the charity, and determine its policies. There are, however, many, many forms of local group structure, some purely for fundraising, some purely for carrying out the programme of the organisation. Their relationship with the charities' fundraising departments varies equally; but there are few local groups that are not encouraged to undertake specific fundraising activities which are supported by the centre, sometimes in a charity week allowing the national organisation to use national publicity to support local fundraising.

With a local group background, all other routes can still be pursued, but the immediate level of entry would be as a local groups' fundraising officer. This would usually require a few years' experience and should be bolstered by undertaking appropriate courses.

The commercial route

At the other extreme, charities are increasingly drawing in people who have worked for both advertising agencies and commercial direct marketing companies. It is preferable, if not essential, of course, to have worked for charity clients in those agencies. Again, if this experience is expanded by fundraising courses or by volunteer work, that helps to build an impressive CV, and this will bring you to the interview. Your CV will need to be good, because in the current market there are often more than 200 applicants for any charity position. Naturally, a business qualification of almost any sort, from OND Business Studies to MBA, also helps.

The larger charities often have posts for advertising managers, direct mail officers, direct response officers, etc., all of which can be approached through this route. It would be unusual to move directly from a commercial company to become the head of a fundraising department, but this does happen, and commercial experience of managing a team is a very useful attribute. It is more usual for the directors of charities to be drawn from the business world by charity councils eager to instil commercial reality into the management and development of charities' incomes.

For specific fundraising positions there are many obvious commercial parallels. Work in a charity shops chain will be accessible to those with similar commercial experience; the merchandise catalogue of a charity needs just the same skills as its commercial partner; and the talents needed to raise money by a host of other means have their commercial equivalents. In fact, charity work often requires both much more sensitivity, e.g. in telemarketing, and a much harder commercial edge, because competition is very tough and you are asking people to give money away, not to buy a product they need.

The training route

This is becoming the most frequent way by which people choose to become a professional fundraiser. Most applicants favouring this route already have degrees, often in subjects relevant to the charities' work, or, more importantly, in a commercial discipline; but they augment this by undertaking both a period of volunteering and a foundation course with the ICFM, and subsequently a series of courses on specific topics with either the ICFM or the Directory of Social Change. This whole bevy of certificates and diplomas can only be beaten by experience, and that, preferably, with a major charity.

If you are going down this route, then it pays to be selective, dovetailing the courses you take to the position you are after. If you intend to move up the career ladder, from assistant to member of a fundraising department, to Head of Fundraising, to becoming a director, then no specialism must be maintained for long. A head of department will usually have a specialist knowledge of the direct response industry, because that is where most of the income will probably come from, but that is by no means universally true.

One of the best places to start your training is with the Open University. This allows you the luxury of working in one job whilst acquiring the skills necessary for the next. The list of useful organisations at the end of this book has the addresses of the principal organisations mentioned above, which offer training courses. Write or phone them for a current list of courses on offer.

The external environment is changing so rapidly for fundraisers, as for everyone else, that it has become commonplace to say that your training will never stop.

Changing jobs

It is more likely that you will find your next job outside your current charity. Promotion is by no means assured, and a charity career is a rocky one, as charities rise and fall in the same way as other businesses. Often the breakthrough to promotion will come from your Rolodex of business cards and contacts and you should cultivate with great care your contacts in other organisations.

Make sure your triumphs are known outside your current employment, and make good use of the charity press to advertise yourself. The charity press often seems to be growing daily and *Professional Fundraising, The Third Sector* and *Charity* are all widely read. In the US the *Chronicle of Philanthropy* has a large circulation. There are also various bulletin boards opening up on the Internet which make interesting reading. They tend to be based on the US not-for-profit sector, but will give an interesting insight into their methods and could even lead to your next position.

Changing charities

It may be a wrench for you to think of leaving your favourite charity to improve your prospects, but once that challenge is taken, it is usually seen that there are many organisations with equally important claims to a healthy income. Causes are often more interlinked than it first appears from the confines of your first charity. Changing charities also gives a breadth of experience that will enhance both your everyday work and your future prospects.

The changing profession

In the past few years fundraising has really taken off as a profession, acquiring a respect that many other professions seem determined to lose. Fundraising departments have grown rapidly in many organisations, developing a set of fundraising managers and directors who were scarce on the ground not so long ago. The latest trend has been international, with an increasing number of fundraising managers training the overseas branches of international charities to fundraise in their own countries. These glamorous international fundraisers hold aspirational positions that require great experience, cultural adaptability, entrepreneurial spirit, a love of airports and laptop computers, and the ability to function in all temperatures without sleep!

The challenge of fundraising in every possible environment has reinvigorated many organisations. At one extreme, as the newly industrialised countries of the Pacific Rim emerge, there are fundraisers tapping into the wealth being created there, especially western university fundraisers following their affluent alumni back home. At the other, there are fundraisers in the very poorest countries, locating the inevitable class of rich and affluent people and going to work on them.

§

Fundraising is one of the key professions for building a better world. It has the power to transform societies and the way they operate. It can take the dreams of thousands of individually powerless donors and turn them into a force for positive change. I hope that this book will help to make your work for such changes more effective.

Ten Principles Of Fundraising

1. The Pareto principle

80% of your income can come from 20% of your supporters. Learn who they are, develop the relationship, and approach them for more until the ratio comes true.

2. 'My friend the fundraiser'

People give to people, not to organisations. They give to help end suffering, so in your fundraising bring them as close to the victims as possible but become their friend in the process, and build up the relationship for long-term giving.

3. 'Thank you!'

Always say 'thank you', and say it promptly. It is a common courtesy and shows respect for your donors and gratitude for their generosity. If you do not say 'thank you' you do not deserve another donation. Thanking people helps to cement your friendship. Do not try to get out of it.

4. How much?

Always let people know how much you would like them to give. It makes them feel comfortable and makes you look competent. If there is no indication of the amount you need people worry that they may be thought foolish for giving away a lot, or mean for giving just a little. Whilst they deliberate the immediacy goes out of your request, and you may lose the donation altogether.

5. Testing, testing, testing

Until you test, you do not know. You can have a hundred theories about your fundraising programme and your donors, but until you actually run one idea against another you do not really know which one works. It is easy to do in some cases, such as direct mail, and harder in others, such as advertising - but is essential in all cases. Always try to learn something each time you carry out an idea, and always test ideas on the smallest statistically relevant sample possible.

6. The myth of the Magic Lunch

It is said there are no free lunches. Yet we tend to believe that our supporters give us money and receive nothing in return. Is this true? Just what do they receive? What happens at the magic lunch? If you cannot answer these questions, ask people. If you do not know why they support you, you cannot fundraise effectively and efficiently.

7. The product cycle

All products, including your fundraising devices, go through cycles. In the early days they will be costly as you learn and test in small quantities; then, when the formula is working, the money will roll in - but after a while the market will be saturated, the public will tire of your approach, or you will just appear old-fashioned and irrelevant. Be prepared for this and prepared to respond rapidly to such changes. In some cases you can revamp your appeal. In others your organisation will need a radically new approach. For example, there are signs that common-interest groups are replacing local groups, so organisations dependent on local groups should consider restructuring based on professional classes.

8. Make it easy

Surprisingly, the least effort can put people off giving. They are well intentioned, but if they have to find a stamp the desire to give will have gone long before the stamp turns up. Use FREEPOST envelopes, print the donor's name and address for them, fill out their bank details, ring them up and remind them - it all helps more than you would imagine.

9. 'We're different.'

When I worked for Oxfam, people told me that it was hard to fundraise because people liked to give to local organisations like Friends of the Earth. When I worked for Friends of the Earth people told me all the money goes to people, not the planet, and it was easy for organisations like Amnesty International. At Amnesty it has been said that Oxfam has an easy time fundraising for disasters. When I went to India... Yes, it will work for you. No, it's not easy.

10. The truth

Always tell the truth. Do not be tempted to make your case stronger than it is. If your organisation makes a mistake or things go wrong, do not hide it. The press is waiting for charities to slip up. Nothing makes a better press story than a saint who has sinned.

Useful Books

The Voluntary Sector Legal Handbook
Adirondack, Sandy & Taylor, Sinclair James
Directory of Social Change (DSC), 1996, ISBN 1 873860 79 X

Charity Appeals
Allford, Marion
Dent/Institute of Charity Fundraising Managers (ICFM), 1993, ISBN 0 460 86191 3

Relationship Fundraising
Burnett, Ken
White Lion Press, 1992, ISBN 0 9518971 0 1

A Guide to the Major Trusts, Vol. II
Casson, David
DSC, 1995/96 , ISBN 1 873860 64 1

Directory of Grant-making Trusts
Charities Aid Foundation (CAF), 1996, ISBN 0 904757 994

Grants from Europe
Davidson, Ann,
National Council for Voluntary Organisations (NCVO), 1993, ISBN 0 7199 1382 9

Guide to Company Giving
Ed. Casson, David,
DSC, 1995, ISBN 1 873860 31 5

The Arts Funding Guide
Doulton, Anne-Marie (ed.)
DSC, 1994, ISBN 1 873860 31 5

The Central Government's Grants Guide
Doulton, Anne-Marie
DSC, 1995, ISBN 1 873860 73 0

EU Research Funding - a guide for applicants
Commission of the European Communities
London Office, 8 Storey's Gate, London SW1P 3AT.

Marketing on the Internet
Ellsworth, Jill & Matthew,
Wiley, 1995, ISBN 0 471 11850 8

Hollis Sponsorship and Donations Yearbook
Hollis Directories Ltd., 1996, ISBN 0 900 96755 2

Guide to the National Lottery
Hurd, Howard
1995, ISBN 1 873860 67 6

A Guide to the Major Trusts Vol. I
FitzHerbert, Luke
1995/96 , ISBN 1 873860 49 8

Networking in Europe
NCVO, 1995, ISBN 0 7199 1460

The Borderless World
Ohmae, Kenichi
HarperCollins, 1994, SBN 0 00 638364 5

Ogilvy on Advertising
Ogilvy, David
Guild Publishing, 1985

The Tom Peters Seminar: Crazy Times call for Crazy Organisations
Peters, Tom
Macmillan, 1994, ISBN 0 333 62864 0

Maverick
Semler, Ricardo
Century, 1993, ISBN 0 7126 5451 8

The International Foundation Directory
Hodson, H. V. (Ed.)
Europa Publications, ISBN 0 46653 66 6

Peace and International Relations
Forrester, Susan
DSC, 1994, ISBN 1 873860 58 7

The Foundation Directory
Stan Olson (Ed.)
The Foundation Centre, New York

US Foundation Support in Europe 1994/5
Ruth Lauer & Steve England (Eds.)
The Directory of Social Change, ISBN 1 873860 34 X

Fundraising on the Internet
Lake, Howard
Aurelian, 1996, ISBN 1 899247 06 8

Useful Organisations

NCVO (National Council for Voluntary Organisations)

On its World Wide Web pages the NCVO describes itself thus: 'The NCVO is a membership organisation of national and voluntary organisations. We have some 650 members ranging from helplines to large household name charities. Our mission is to work to support the voluntary sector as well as to work to improve its effectiveness. We are known as 'the voice of the voluntary sector' for our work in supporting the needs of charities. We provide a range of services to our members such as fundraising or financial advice, and also campaign on issues affecting voluntary organisations as a whole, such as the impact of Value Added Tax or the National Lottery. Our magazine, *NCVO News*, provides up-to-date information about developments in the charity world and also a range of features about the key issues and personalities. We welcome new members, who are eligible for discounts on our services and are able to participate in discussions on policies affecting the future of charities.' Much more is available.

ICFM (Institute of Charity Fundraising Managers)

The ICFM's Mission Statement: The Institute and its Trust (a registered charity) promote the highest standards of fundraising.

The Institute represents the interests of its members and, through its charitable trust, aims to further knowledge, skills and effectiveness in all aspects of fundraising practice. It fulfils its mission by developing standards of good fundraising practice which encompass strict adherence to law, appropriate ethical practice in relation to the cause for which support is sought, public accountability and respect for the rights and wishes of both donors and clients.

The ICFM Codes of Practice (which every fundraiser should follow) are:

- Guidance Notes and Standard Form of Contract for dealing with Consultants
- ICFM Consultants List. Codes of Practice on Lotteries, Reciprocal Mailings, Schools
- Telephone Recruitment of Collectors and the Scottish Code of Fundraising Practice.

There are new codes of practice on Static Collection Boxes, Outbound Telephone Support, and House to House Collections. All these are available for a small fee from the ICFM.

Useful Addresses

Advertising Standards Authority (ASA)

2-16 Torrington Place, London, WC1E 7HN.
Tel: 0171 580 5555

Angal

68 First Avenue, Mortlake, London SW14 8SR.
Tel: 0181 788 5464
Manufactures collecting boxes, etc.

Arts Council of England, Lottery Department

14 Great George Street, London SW1P 3NQ.
Tel: 0171 312 0123

British Council, Central Information Point

10 Spring Gardens, London SW1A 2BN
Tel: 0171 839 4382
Youth exchange grants, cultural relations policy etc.

Business in the Community

227A City Road, London, EC1V 1JV.
Encourages community involvement in job creation and corporate responsibility,
and administers the One Per Cent Club.

CAFOD (Catholic Fund for Overseas Development)

2 Romero Close, Stockwell Road, London SW9 9TY
Tel: 0171-733 7900.

Central Bureau for Educational Visits and Exchanges

Management Services and Public Relations Department, Seymour Mews House, Seymour Mews, London W1H 9PE.

Tel: 0171-486 5101

The national information source for educational visits and exchanges.

Charities Aid Foundation

King's Hill, West Malling, Kent, ME19 4TA.

Tel: 01732 520 000

Publishes *Directory of Grant Making Trusts*, runs charity voucher scheme, administers covenants, gives advice to charities on tax etc.

Charities Advisory Trust

Radius Works, Back Lane, London, NW3 1HL.

Tel: 0171 794 9835

For charity trading advice.

Charity Appointments

3 Spital Yard, London, E1 6 AQ

Tel: 0171 247 4502

Helps charities fill key jobs.

Charity Commission

St Albans House, 57-60 Haymarket, London, SW1Y 4QX

Tel: 0171 210 4477

Graeme House, Derby Square, Liverpool L2 7SB

Tel: 0151 227 3919

Woodfield House, Tangier, Taunton, Somerset TA1 4BL

Tel: 01823 345000

Registers and regulates charities.

Charity Recruitment

40 Rosebery Avenue,London EC1R 4RN

Tel. 0171 833 0770

Charity recruitment agency

Commission of the European Communities

8 Storey's Gate, London, SW1P 3AT

Tel: 0171 973 1992, Fax: 0171 973 1900

The Commission itself is at Rue de la Loi 200, 1049 Brussels, Belgium, Tel: + 32 2 299 1111.

Data Protection Registrar

Information Services Department, Wycliffe House, Water Lane, Wilmslow, Cheshire SK9 5AF, Tel: 01625 535 777, Fax: 01625 524510

Registers users of personal information held electronically

Department of Employment

ESF Section, 236 Gray's Inn Road, London WC1X 8HL

Tel: 0171-211 4732

For information on the European Social Fund

Department of the Environment

Environmental Protection, Central Division, Room A132, Romney House, 43 Marsham Street SW1P 3AT,

Tel: 0171-276 8146.

UK Government department dealing with environmental protection.

Department of Trade and Industry

Investment and Development Division, 232 Kingsgate House, 66-74 Victoria Street, London SW1E 6SW

Tel: 0171-636 2556

For advice on the European Regional Development Fund

Directorate-General V

Employment and Social Affairs, Room 921, Adelphi, 1-11 John Adam Street, London WC2N 6HT Tel: 0171-962 8411.

C4 Avenue de Cortenburg, 1040 Brusselss

Tel: +32 2 735 1671

EU Directorate responsible for European Social Fund, Health and Safety at Work etc. London address for information.

Directorate-General X

Women's Information Service, Communication and Culture, Rue de la Loi 200, 1049 Brussels

Tel: + 322 299 1111

EU Directorate for Women's Information Service etc.

Directorate-General X

Audio Visual, Information, Communication and Culture, Rue de la Loi 200, 1049 Brussels

Tel: + 32 2 299 9366

EU Directorate for audio-visual media etc.

Directory of Social Change

24 Stephenson Way, London NW1 2DP

Tel: 0171 209 4422

Great book list and fundraising courses.

European Environmental Bureau

Rue de la Victoire, 1060 Brussels

Tel: + 32 2 539 0037

Provides information and represents NGO members' interests.

ExecuCare

Collier House, 163-169 Brompton Rd., London SW3 1PY

Tel.0171 589 4567

Charity recruitment agency.

Forster Munroe

13-27 Brunswick Place, London N1 6DX

Tel: 0171 251 4890, Fax: 0171 251 4860

'*Alms*' computer database software supplier for charities.

Halfpenny Press

Caxton House, Holbrook, Ipswich, Suffolk IP9 2QS.

Tel: 01473 328400

Specialist printers of raffle tickets etc.

Hollis Sponsorship and Donation Yearbook

Contact House, Lower Hampton Road, Sunbury-on-Thames, Middlesex, TW16 5HG

Tel: 0181 977 7711 Fax:0181 977 1133

Human Rights Foundation

13 Rue Van Campenhout, 1040 Brussels

Tel: + 32 2 299 3243

For the promotion of human rights. Also small grants for innovatory projects worldwide.

HMSO

St Crispins, Duke Street, Norwich, NR3 1PD.

Tel: 01603 622211

HMSO Bookshop

41 High Holborn, London, WC1V 6HB.

You can obtain copies of the new Charities Act from either address.

Inland Revenue Claims Branch

St John's House, Merton Road, Bootle L69 9BB

Considers claims for tax exemption.

Institute of Charity Fundraising Managers

208 Market Towers, Nine Elms Lane, London SW8 5NQ

Tel: 0171 627 3436

The professional association for all fundraisers and consultants. Sets standards, runs courses, etc.

Institute of Personnel Managers

IPM House, Camp Road, Wimbledon, London SW19 4UW.

Advice and codes of conduct on personnel matters.

International Fund Raising Group

295 Kennington Road, London, SE11 4QE.

Tel: 0171 587 0287

Organises fundraising workshops globally, including the major annual European workshop in the Netherlands.

John Rodd & Associates

Coombe House, Stoke Hill, Chew Stoke, Bristol BS18 8XF.

Tel: 01761 221702

Helps you get the computer database advice you always wanted.

Japan Business Consultancy

19 Somerset Place, Bath, BA1 5SF,

Tel: 01225 444190

For advice on working with Japanese companies in the UK.

JETRO (Japanese External Trade Organisation)

Publications Department, 2-5 Toranomon 2-Chome, Minatu-Ku,Tokyo 105, Japan.

For information on Japanese companies.

King Baudouin Foundation

21 Brederostraat, 1000 Brussels
Tel: + 32 2 511 1840.
Some grants for projects related to social issues and the environment in Europe.

Millennium Commission

2, Little Smith Street, London, SW1P 3DH
Tel: 0171 340 2001
Administers the Millenium Fund

National Council for Voluntary Organisations

Regent's Wharf, 8 All Saints Street, London N1 9RL.
Tel: 0171 713 6161.
Represents and advises NGOs on a wide variety of issues.

National Heritage Memorial Fund

Heritage Lottery Fund, 10 St James' Street, London SW1A 1EF.
Tel: 0171 747 2087/6/5/4/3/2

National Lottery Charities Board

7th Floor, St Vincent House, 30 Orange Street, London, WC2H 7HH
Tel: 0345 919191
Administers the Lottery fund for charities.

Paul Barker Consultancy

4 Verney House, 1B Hollywood Road, London SW10 9HS.
Tel: 0171 376 5322
Great direct mail agency.

The Razor's Edge

GFI Solutions Ltd, FREEPOST, The Claremont Centre, 39 Durham St.,Glasgow G41 1BR.

Tel: 0141 427 7939, Fax: 0141 427 1413.

Supplier of the computer database software *'The Razor's Edge'*.

Smee & Ford

2nd Floor, St George's House, 195/203 Waterloo Road, London SE1 8XJ.

Tel: 0171 928 4050.

Runs a will reporting service for charities and much more.

Sports Council National Lottery Unit

PO Box 649, London WC1H 0QP

Tel: 0171 388 1277 and 0345 649649 (Lottery line).

Index